ESP32
COOKBOOK

ESP8266, Arduino Coding, Example Code, IoT Project, Sensors, Esp32 Startup

By

Janani Sathish

TABLE OF CONTENTS

WHAT IS ESP 32? 5

INTRODUCTION TO ESP8266 AND ESP32 11

SYSTEM SOFTWARE ON ESP8266 AND ESP32 14

DOWNLOAD AND INSTALL ARDUINO ESP AND USB DRIVER 16

DOWNLOAD AND INSTALL ARDUINO ESP32 V1 DEVELOPMENT ENVIRONMENT 20

DOWNLOAD AND INSTALL ARDUINO PRO IDE 23

DOWNLOAD AND INSTALL ARDUINO ESP AND USB DRIVER 26

DOWNLOAD AND INSTALL ARDUINO ESP32 V1 DEVELOPMENT ENVIRONMENT 30

LOAD YOUR FIRST CODE TO THE ESP32 BOARD 33

HELLO WORLD ON ESP32 36

HELLO WORLD ON ESP32 - PART2 42

HELLO WORLD ON ESP32 - PART3 47

ESP32 STARTUP 51

HELLO WORLD PROJECT STRUCTURE 57

EXAMPLE CODE 59

PROGRAMMING WITHOUT CODING SOFTWARE 62

DOWNLOAD AND INSTALL PROGRAMMING SOFTWARE 63

DOWNLOAD AND INSTALL ARDUINO IDE 66

DOWNLOAD AND INSTALL ARDUINO ESP AND USB DRIVER 70

ESP 32 PINOUT V1 DOIT 74

WHAT IS THE ESP32 BOARD 78

DOWNLOAD AND INSTALL ARDUINO ESP32 V1 DEVELOPMENT ENVIRONMENT 79

USER INTERFACE 82

USER INTERFACE IN DETAILS 85

EXAMPLE BLINK LED WITH ONE CLICK	97
UPLOAD BLINK LED CODE AND TEST IT	100
ARDUINO IDE INSTALLATION	103
ESP-IDF INSTALLATION	107
WIFI SNIFFER - 1	111
WIFI SNIFFER - 2	117
WIFI SNIFFER - 3	122
EXAMPLE CODE	127
OLED ESP32 DISPLAY PART1	133
ESP32 DISPLAY PART2	136
OLED ESP32 DISPLAY PART3	138
EXAMPLE CODE	139
CREATE A NEW EMAIL ACCOUNT TO BE USED AS SENDER	147
SMTP SERVER SETTINGS	149
CODING THE ESP32 EMAIL ALERT PROJECT	150
EXAMPLE CODE	161
PRACTICAL TESTING	163
SENSOR ALERT VIA EMAIL	166
CONTROLLED WITH A BUTTON	171
UPLOAD BUTTON CODE AND TEST IT	172
PRACTICAL EXAMPLE INFRARED OBSTACLE AVOIDANCE SENSOR	173
LED BAR COUNTER ENCODER SHIFT REGISTER	175
TORQUE DESIGN CONCEPTS	184
Selection Components for the Design	186
UNDERSTANDING ELECTRONIC SUPPLY	191
CALCULATING REQUIRED TORQUE FOR MOTORS	194
ROBOTIC ARM THEORETICAL UNDERSTANDING	197

3D MODELING AND BUILDING THE ROBOT 200

TESTING SERVO MOTORS 204

UNDERSTANDING PICK AND PLACE BEHAVIOR 206

PROGRAMMING PICK AND THROW 208

OPTIMIZE ROBOTS MOTION 212

TRANSFORMATION MATRICES 214

UNDERSTANDING THE APPLICATION OF TRANSFORMATION MATRICES
.... 217

INTRODUCTION WITH EXAMPLE 220

DERIVING DH TABLE FOR OUR ROBOT 224

1-DOF KINEMATIC ANALYSIS 227

KINEMATIC SOLUTIONS THROUGH PYTHON LIBRARIES 230

IMPLEMENTING FORWARD KINEMATICS 2-DOF 242

IMPLEMENTING FORWARD KINEMATICS 3-DOF 245

ESP32 WIFI WEATHER STATION PROJECT WITH A NEXTION DISPLAY
AND A BME280 SENSOR 248

WHAT IS ESP 32?

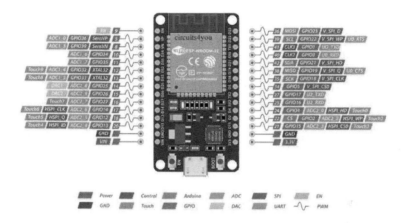

The ESP32 development board, which was released as a successor to the ESP8266 chip, made a huge impact on the IoT industry as it integrated Bluetooth with WiFi and utilized a dual-core processor.

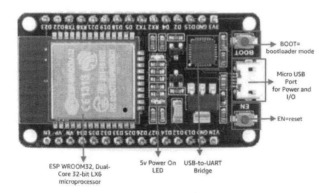

ESP32-S3 is the latest addition to Espressif's microcontroller series, specifically designed for IoT applications. In this video, we will look into the specifications of ESP32-S3 and its applications. Espressif announced the ESP32-S3 microcontroller on 1st December 2020. It features a dual-core Xtensa LX7 CPU, while its previous iteration, the ESP32-S2, was based on a single-core Xtensa LX7 CPU.

ESP8266   **ESP32**

The S2 model was considered a bridge between the ESP8266 and ESP32 microcontrollers regarding performance and cost. For more details on ESP32-S2, check out our previous video in the link provided below. The

latest version gets a significant boost in performance and retains the improved hardware-level security of the S2 family. It also includes other features of the ESP32-S2, such as USB On-The-Go support and an improved touchpad sensor implementation. Now, let us have a detailed overview of the features. The ESP32-S3 has 384 KB of RAM and an additional 512 KB of SRAM. The dual-core CPU has a clock speed of up to 240 MHz. It comes built-in with 2.4 GHz, 802.11 b/g/n WiFi, and 40 MHz of bandwidth support. It features Bluetooth Low Energy 5.0 connectivity capable of long-range communication over 1 km through the coded PHY layer. it also supports higher transmission speeds and data throughput with 2 Mbps transfer support. An impressive feature of the ESP32-S3 is that both WiFi and BLE have superior RF performance even at high temperatures. The ESP32-S3 has a total of 44 programmable GPIO pins,

which is ten more than that of the ESP32-S2, and it supports a rich set of peripherals like SP, I2C, UART, I2S, PWM, RMT, ADC, DAC, SD/MMC host and TWAI. 14 GPIO pins can be configured for HMI or Human Machine Interface applications.

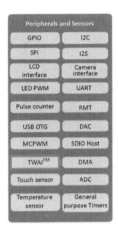

Also, the chip comes with an ultra-low-power (ULP) core that supports multiple low-power modes. The ESP32-S3 is made very secure as it

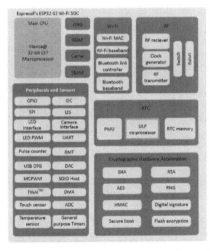

supports AES-XTS-based flash encryption, RSA-based secure boot, digital signature, and HMAC. It also has a "world controller" peripheral that implements a trusted execution environment by providing two fully isolated execution environments. A major highlight of the ESP32-S3 would be its powerful AI acceleration features and support for AIoT applications. The term AIoT stands for Artificial Intelligence plus the Internet of Things. With the vast amount of data collected from IoT devices, the future of AI-based applications looks promising. AI is indeed the key factor in unlocking IoT's full potential. Major AIoT markets include wearables, smart industry, smart home, and smart city sectors. The Xtensa LX7 core has been extended with vector instructions. Vector instructions are essentially a class of instructions that enable parallel processing of AI datasets, thereby improving performance and power efficiency. Such instructions can be leveraged for digital signal processing and neural network computing. Developers at Espressif are currently working on updates for the ESP-WHO library for face detection and the ESP-Skainet library for voice recognition. However, the code for ESP32-S3 SoC is still a work in progress and is not ready for the public yet.

ESP32-S3 speech recognition demo
in a noisy environment

Espressif has released a video demonstration of the speech recognition capabilities of ESP32-S3 using Amazon's built-in Alexa Voice Service (AVS) with blind source separation (BSP) and acoustic echo cancellation (AEC) features. The fact that there are no external DSP chips interfaced with ESP32 proves how powerful it is for AIoT applications. Check out the video demo in the link provided below. Espressif's IoT Development Framework or ESP-IDF also provides support for the ESP32-S3 model.

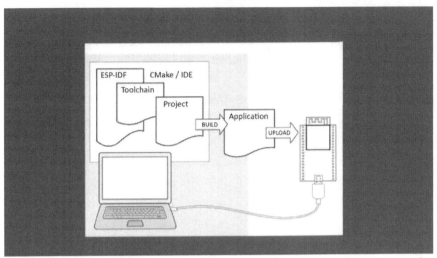

The platform has rigorous testing features for building applications, and it also has a great support policy as it gets frequent updates. Developers can easily migrate their applications to the ESP32-S3 platform and continue working with popular ESP-IDF tools. With support for such libraries in the future, AI applications like object detection and image recognition will be easier to implement with the ESP32-S3. . To conclude, the ESP32-S3 can be regarded as an optimized microcontroller with improved connectivity, AI processing power, and support for commonly used peripheral interfaces. The official datasheet for the ESP32-S3 will be released in the next few days, and the market availability date is expected to be announced soon.

INTRODUCTION TO ESP8266 AND ESP32

So we talk about ESB 32 and ESB a 2 6 6. These are system on chips Associates provided by the fabulous semiconductor expressive from China. They are so low cost to use they consist of the Wi-Fi and the dual-mode Bluetooth classic and Beasley and allows us to build Internet of Things applications. I wrote the applications in a very cheap manner. These are both out of less than 10 dollars in cost so they're very cheap and they're very easy to bring up and write applications on. So again as I mentioned designed by the Chinese fabulous semiconductor company called expressive fabulous means that they just create the chip design and other companies take these chip designs on paper and manufacture the silicon right. So what is great about this is that it's very cheap. It has a very simple cedar link to control the MCU and passes 80 commands to control the MCU to sort of start and stop communications to connect to Wi-Fi and so on. So it's very easy to use and very cheap for us to build out the applications. So talking about the ESB 8 2 6 6 hardware it's built with the one CPO which is the 32-bit risk microprocessor L1 0 6. It has 32 kilobytes of instruction ram it has some user data RAM as I mentioned here 80 kilobytes. It has an SBA-based flash you can go up to 16 15 megabytes bunch of GPI opens allows us to connect LCD and other sensors to it and other things on this list in terms of RAM it has 160 kilobytes of the ram of it. We have 64 kilobytes of instruction RAM and 96 kilobytes of data Ram. You can be going to store in the data the item of 64 kilobytes for the partition into two blocks of 32 kilobytes. One is for the ram that the program uses another is the cache which is the cache from the flash memory so when you write a sketch and as the code executes and finds out that that piece of code is in the flash it sort of catches that piece of code from the flash into this piece of RAM and executes from the RAM. Yeah, there's a flash memory but you can store the sketch file and the images they are. That is an external flash memory that doesn't come inside the associate and it's connected to the chip by the SBA bus and can be as big as 16 megabytes in the ESB 8 2 6 6. The Flash is statically created and at fixed addresses with an ESB 32 flash is divided into sections of partitions and stored at a fixed address and you can read the partition table and add more partitions and put other kinds of data on this partition table. As I mentioned earlier both of these associates can execute code directly from flash but over because that is slow. What usually happens is that it is catching to some addresses into RAM and executed from the RAM. This is the flash memory layout for the ESB 8 2 6 6. You have the sketch that you wrote in Arduino or some other idea that comes and this piece of code. You can also have another piece of foam there that you can download over the ear called the Audio update that sits around this location and also a very basic file system. You can go in stores on files like HDMI files and then stuff like that and it has an E from the sector and also some Wi-Fi contribution database where you control your society across reboots which is very helpful this is the block diagram of the ESB 8 2 6 6. If you notice this is the part which is the Wi-Fi. And this is the part which is the all your seat using and registers and stuff and you have the onboard antenna. This is a general layout of the ESB 8 2 6 expense providing a lot of data in GPI Europeans and there's also ground and voltage provider so you can look up in other places also but generally want to show it do you here for completeness. Yes, 32 is a dual-core processor compared to ESB 8 2 6 6 which allows us a lot more flexibility in terms of not having to yield in our programs not having to care to might we're taking too much time on one processor. So because if two microprocessors and you have a free art was always running on these two microprocessors you can write that well. I mean the way you'd only write Linux programs and the free autos takes care of ensuring that all the processes and threads that you're running are do get their time on it. So these two processes are called protocols CPE was an application CPE was and you could have one of these you would just handle the Wi-Fi Bluetooth and DCP IP and stuff and the other app CPE were left for application code is really up to you and how you manage your processes might be hot. This ESB 32 runs the free autos SDK whereas the ESB 8 2 6 6 had a choice of both non OS SDK which is just a shim layer of callback functions as well as the free outdoor sport but it needs to be 30. You just have the ESB IDF as a framework that runs on free or DOS the hardware is much more detailed you have much more memory in it and many more GPA opens it's a 48 bean so see what are the 32 pin office be 32 so it gives you much more control. It also has Bluetooth in it vs. the ESB a two-sixes that only had the Wi-Fi that had both Bluetooth and Wi-Fi built into the sea. And this is the block diagram where you have the radio portion is here and you also have some crypto graphic hardware theory and explanation modules like E S and stuff that you can do in hardware. You also have an ultra-low-power local processor that you can use for somebody low sort of intensity things like in a deep sleep. You can have this guy wake up and just make sure that the Wi-Fi is up or so on. So you have an option of one more processor here and you are many more kinds of interfaces. Also some sensors built-in like that sensor and how sensors temperature sensors are built into the SCC is very interesting from an eye out perspective. OK. Quickly about modules and boards so ESB 8 0 6 6 and 32 comes to involve associate chip that we just mentioned above that you could have ESB modules or ESB Dev boards. So module boards don't have the connections for peripheral they just throw simple modules that can be used by board manufacturers. The modules come from various manufacturers. Expressive itself gives you modules for ESB 8 to 6 6 Scalia's BW R O M 0 2 and S2. You also have another company called E I think that also makes modules called ESB 0 1 to ESB 14 whereas for ESB 32 again you have people making modules like I think are expressive and others. These modules that I've done use by board manufacturers to go and put most. It's a more sort of sensors and connections over them and that's in the next light. So here are the development boards that are built using those modules they put up a node MCU by I think or uses that ESB twelve module to make a board and get SB 32. Again you have these boards that are built by oppressive expressive as well as other companies here even though the modules that expressive themselves built of it can be picked up by board manufacturers to build boards around the ESB 32 K K that's all for now

SYSTEM SOFTWARE ON ESP8266 AND ESP32

We're gonna talk about the systems outfit that is run on ESB 8 2 6 6 and ESB 32 that enables you to write software application programs on these two sources. So one of the first waves which is sort of an easy way to write your applications on these two chipsets is to use the knowledge as the IDC. Now if you're using the ESB 8 2 6 6 it comes in two flavors. You can either use a non OS SDK from a suppressive which is layered or what the associate and above this you have the audio Shim layer which provides its API is like set up and loop and you can write your application programs the way you understand it as you write today on ordinal and you can write your programs and they will run on this non our dos as D.K. from expressive on ESB 8 2 6 6. Similarly on the ESB 32 also you have the ordinary ported within specimens provided an ESB IDF which is called an I O T document framework that runs on the ESB 32 and above this you have the Arduino Shim layer where again you can write application programs using the API provided by the ordinal which again has a set up and loop routines and and you can have programs that run on both 8 2 6 6 and 32 using arduino as the ITC the non OS SDK and we're talking about ESB 8 2 6 6 is basically it is not an operating system is just a shim layer that provides you timers and callbacks and like an event loop which also has the ESB con network interface that allows you to write programs and uses API is to write your application programs the anon with SDK is just run or the native hardware and the user programs are sort of responsible for their proper execution of the code because you know the at the dictates of doesn't provide you any task scheduling like standard are dos always as do the non with as Dicky also does not preempt your tasks so you have to be careful if you are running task you have to call the yield function so that the other tasks such as taking care of Wi-Fi or DCP IP sort of get a chance to run. Otherwise you'll see that infamous error called W W to reset which sort of goes and resets your ESB 8 to 6 6 or 3 2 or 3 to chipset if you don't give time for system critical functions through to run so so then always has decay in a sense for you for types of functions the application functions the call back and timer functions that ISIS is and they use the tasks very easy to set up you just go to dyno install it and in the edit references you go and give the ESB 8 2 6 6 3 2 bored you are ill and you don't have good to go whereas if you want to work with the US as decade it needs a bit more of a setup you're not using all you know I D E you have to go and install the free dos manually install the DCC tool chain and then the ESB will not be by utility to which which uploads a phone where and then you can write your software that uses the free autos API is and and you can write like a standard Linux kind of a program which will run on this free toss as decade that is running or what the ESB 8 to 6 6. Similarly, the next version of ESB 8 to 6 it's called the ESB 32 has an OS as decay it doesn't have a non OS SDK it only uses an OS SDK which is again right from the free autos and here we have two ideas. One is we're again well-known order no idea either I mentioned earlier where the audio has what a shim layer above the ESB IDF and you again have your sort of well-known function like setup and loop and you can code the way we normally do for audio or you can let go of audio and you can directly use the ESB IDF as a framework and write code which uses the free autos API directly. So this is these are two methods that we have for ESB 32 so yes we it do again does not use a non with SDK it only has one option to use an OS SDK which is derived from free autos and we have these two famous sorts of frameworks apart from other frameworks that people provide but these do are well known the audio idea and the ESB idea framework. Okay, so that's pretty much it in this.

DOWNLOAD AND INSTALL ARDUINO ESP AND USB DRIVER

Now, listen, it started with a software setup. Hang onto your keyboard and mouse. This part might get bumpy, follow along closely as we configure and upload our first DIY Wi-Fi-connected software. And this lesson will install the E.S.P eight two six six Balde package inside our Arduino software. We will also install a device driver for the Bolt communication chip and upload it on our tweeners kitsch that connects to your home wireless network. The good news is that once you have completed the steps and this and this lesson, you won't have to do them again. You are using the same computer and the same ball. You don't have to reconfigure and reinstall any of the software that we are going to install and the software or in this lesson. So the first step will be installing the undoing of software as your original Arduino software is available for free. On the other Dimino, the S.E.C. website. So the first tab will be going to the ALGUIEN and the S.E.C. go to the software section, click downloads. And from here. Choose your operating system. In our case, it's Windows operating system. We can use Windows installer, all the windows up and I already installed windows up. Here it is.

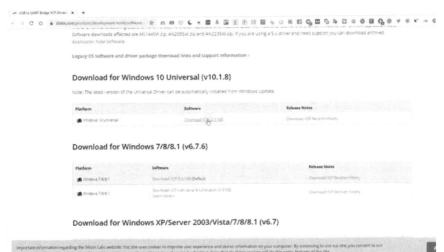

Now, by default, three new application support chips used an official Arduino board, but not that E.S.P board. These boards can be programmed out of the box because the Arduino application already knows about each one and its four abilities. One cool thing about Arduino is that you can add support for other bolts and all you have to do is tell. And we know where to discover their priorities. The first tip of that process is to provide you are to additional boards. Manager. Now. You have to go to the edit, and from there you need to go to the Find menu and select preferences. You will get to see this window, as you can see here. We have additional boards.

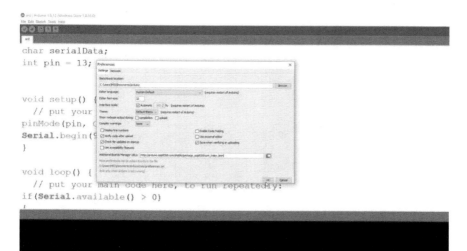

Manager, you are out and you have to base a specific. You are all in that window. I will give it the resources of this project. But here it is. Let me copy and paste that you are on. This is the adrenals E.S.P. You are all for this package. Now, if the box was not blank, where did you open that preferences window? You may have some other box already installed. If that's the case, Ben, the text box content with the above, you are all using a comma to submit a different you are. So you can have this one and add a comma and add another one. But since we only have one, I will base it here. After doing that, click OK to play to close that preferences window. Now are only an application. Knows where to find info about that. Yes. People in general. So let's go to the tools. And from there. Go to the board, Smilodon. And here in The Boss manager, you need to write E.S.P.

Now, as you can see here, we have E.S.P. Eight, two, six. What you need to do is simply click install. It will take some time to download about 34 megabytes of data to the Arduino libraries folder. And once done, it will show you a message indicating that everything is done. Now, once it's done, as you can see, it says in a stall here, you can click close.

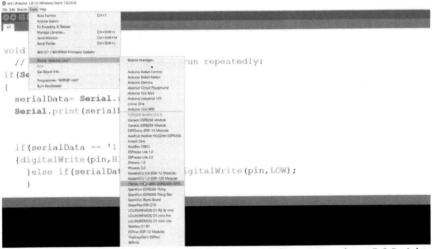

And if you went to the board manager, you can see that now we have E.S.P eight to six, six and E.S.P eight to eight, five and other E.S.P boards. Most of them are here now. What you need to do is simply start using them. And I already mentioned that the one that we have. ATamp; T is the ISP. Further to the eight two six six Modu. Now. To make sure that it's recognized when connecting you are speedboat, you need to install an additional driver from the Sea Lab website. I will give you links to this driver as well. So you need to go and check your operating system. And we have to send your vessel. So we will use this software, click download the VCP.

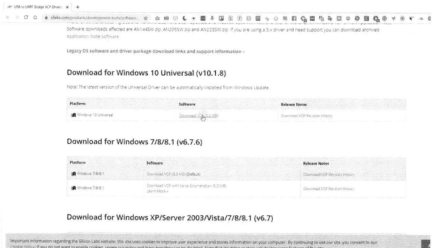

The download will start. You can simply click download. After that, you can install it. The driver, depending on your operating system. That's it. Now, we have installed the Aldwin software that E.S.P library for our Greenall and the ISP driver.

DOWNLOAD AND INSTALL ARDUINO ESP32 V1 DEVELOPMENT ENVIRONMENT

Now, if you have a board like the one that we have, which is E.S.P, first it will vote on one. You need to go to the tools and from the tools menu, you can simply go to the board, select parts manager, and from there. Right, E.S.P. Thirty-two now. If you didn't get any results, you need to do one thing before moving on. You need to add that E.S.P 32 Package Digest's on the file link to the preferences window. So let's go click file.

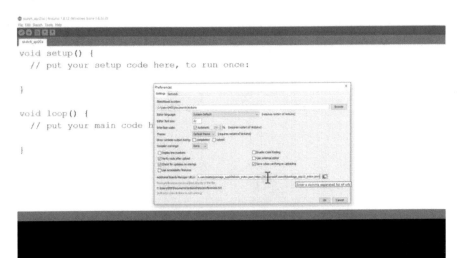

Preferences and here are the comma, then the second length. I'll give you all of these links in the resources project. Again, go to the tools board sports manager and here. Nuccitelli E.S.P. And here it is.

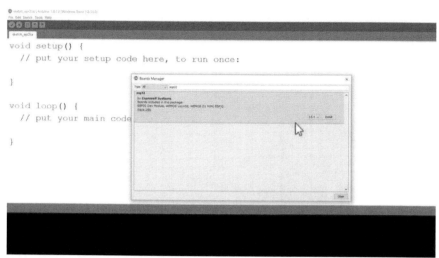

You can simply click install store. This Paul. It will take some time. Now, once you are done, you will see an assault here. Click loans and go to the tools menu. From there, you can check the ball. That's what you want to connect to and you can see that we have.

List of votes down here, you need to choose the one that matches your configuration. In our case. Okay, sorry. Now our case will be DeWit. E.S.P. And we need to choose to do it. E.S.P 32. So let's scroll up. OK, here we have E.S.P, 32 people, kit or AVL kit div module. And we have other E.S.P 32 modules, as you can see here. We need to do it. E.S.P. d'Hiv gets version one, which is the one that we have here and our labs. And we recommend it to everyone who is just getting started on the Internet of Things. So select it, then go. If you didn't see your ball. I have it on my OSPI bought. I have connected the board but I don't see a board here. In that case. You need to download and install this.

You must be to your art bridge driver. Now, not done that matches your operating system. Make sure to write this name. You are searching for it. If your board is E.S.P 32, depending on your board, there are other drivers. So click, download. Again. Click download here. Tech time, double click.

DOWNLOAD AND INSTALL ARDUINO PRO IDE

new as one in which we will talk about that simply and connecting different components. Now after purchasing the components that we mentioned in the previous lesson. You can simply connect them depending on the schematic that I will show you in this lesson to show you the schematic we need first to download a software called sliding it's a software used to connect different elements without possessing them. As you can see this is arguing with Allard. This is the schematic and this is the ABC. Even if you don't have any previous knowledge you can check it out using our profile by searching the education and engineering team. If you faced a problem finding it please drop us a message and we'll be more than happy to help you find it and learn it with a maximum discount. Now click on no direction then click on the download. Choose your abilities system as you can see it's available for Mac Linux and Windows. It's free software.

We need the windows 64-bit virgin as you can see this is the download link so I'll start the download. It's a fine 108 mega 180 megabytes fine so it will take about two minutes to download. Now again if we went back to this page we can see that the software is used to create circuits with different elements. As you can see this is a lead and this is the Arduino Ono.

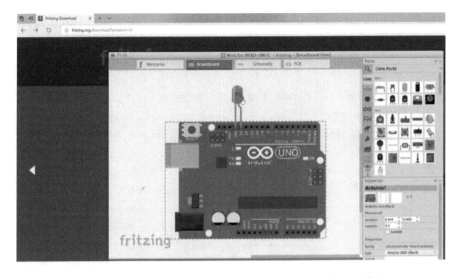

I will take you in a quick tutorial after the software is downloaded on how to use it but it's a very promising software for creating your schematics and creating an ABC design without any complexity, okay I'll bother with you and get back to you once the download is finished again. The software is used to create schematics and to create a PCV. This is before. How would we know? And this is the net that was connected here in this 3D view. So it will make life aware much easier. If you are a university student and you want these images for your presentation you can simply save these designs as be Angie or BBG as an image. It's about saving software of your schematics as images as you can see here. We have a share button.

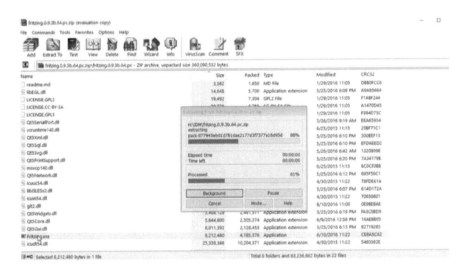

As you can see here click Auburn then you can simply double click the folder go here and turn flights into the XY it's extracting all the files. Let me cancel this and extract it to let's say the documents in a new folder called the slides. Okay. And we can open it using that folder. As you can see this is the folder where we have all the files for the flooding software will take a few minutes it's extracting all of these files since it's dot the I be fine. Okay now let's close this double click on the frightening XY and it will load the items in no time. As you can see k now it's loading the core parts. And as you can see here's the software is loaded.

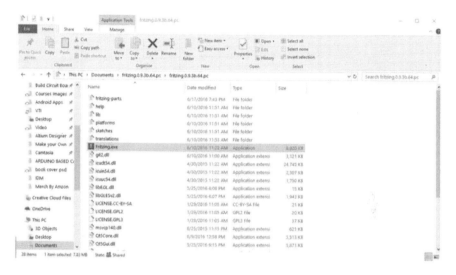

This is the user interface. Here is I will compare the Brit board as you can see schematic B CB and code. Let's create a new file. This is our new fine.

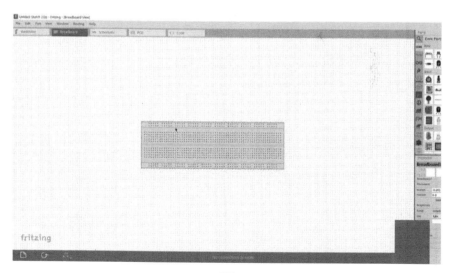

You can search for the items using this search button or you can click on these icons.

DOWNLOAD AND INSTALL ARDUINO ESP AND USB DRIVER

Now, listen, it started with a software setup. Hang onto your keyboard and mouse. This part might get bumpy, follow along closely as we configure and upload our first DIY Wi-Fi-connected software. And this lesson will install the E.S.P eight two six six Balde package inside our Arduino software. We will also install a device driver for the Bolt communication chip and upload it on our tweeners kitsch that connects to your home wireless network. The good news is that once you have completed the steps and this and this lesson, you won't have to do them again. You are using the same computer and the same ball. You don't have to reconfigure and reinstall any of the software that we are going to install and the software or in this lesson. So the first step will be installing the undoing of software as your original Arduino software is available for free. On the other Dimino, the S.E.C. website. So the first tab will be going to the ALGUIEN and the S.E.C. go to the software section, click downloads. And from here. Choose your operating system. In our case, it's Windows operating system. We can use Windows installer, all the windows up and I already installed windows up. Here it is.

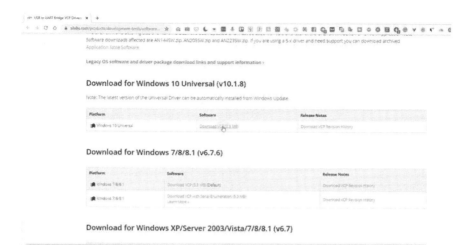

Now, by default, three new application support chips used an official Arduino board, but not that E.S.P board. These boards can be programmed out of the box because the Arduino application already knows about each one and its four abilities. One cool thing about Arduino is that you can add support for other bolts and all you have to do is tell. And we know where to discover their priorities. The first tip of that process is to provide you are to the additional boards. Manager. Now. You have to go to the edit, and from there you need to go to the Find menu and select preferences. You will get to see this window, as you can see here. We have additional boards.

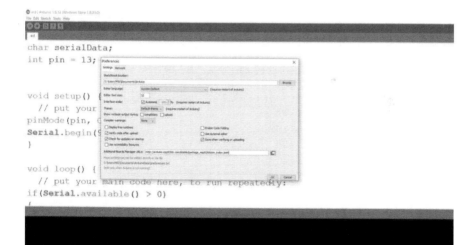

Manager, you are out and you have to base a specific. You are all in that window. I will give it the resources of this project. But here it is. Let me copy and paste that you are on. This is the adrenals E.S.P. You are all for this package. Now, if the box was not blank, where did you open that preferences window? You may have some other box already installed. If that's the case, Ben, the text box content with the above, you are all using a comma to submit a different you are. So you can have this one and add a comma and add another one. But since we only have one, I will base it here. After doing that, click OK to play to close that preferences window. Now are only an application. Knows where to find info about that. Yes. People in general. So let's go to the tools. And from there. Go to the board, Smilodon. And here in The Boss manager, you need to write E.S.P.

Now, as you can see here, we have E.S.P. Eight, two, six. What you need to do is simply click install. It will take some time to download about 34 megabytes of data to the Arduino libraries folder. And once done, it will show you a message indicating that everything is done. Now, once it's done, as you can see, it says in a stall here, you can click close.

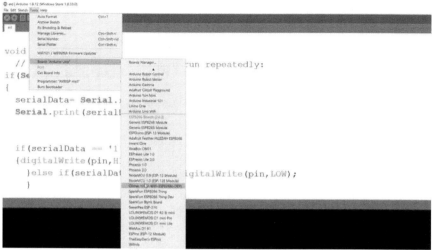

And if you went to the board manager, you can see that now we have E.S.P eight to six, six and E.S.P eight to eight, five and other E.S.P boards. Most of them are here now. What you need to do is simply start using them. And I already mentioned that the one that we have. AT& T is the ISP. Further to the eight two six six Modu. Now. To make sure that it's recognized when connecting you are speedboat, you need to install an additional driver from the Sea Lab website. I will give you links to this driver as well. So you need to go and check your operating system. And we have to send your vessel. So we will use this software, click download the VCP.

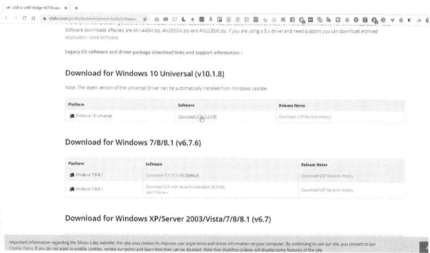

The download will start. You can simply click download. After that, you can install it. The driver, depending on your operating system. That's it. Now, we have installed the Aldwin software that E.S.P library for our Greenall and the ISP driver.

DOWNLOAD AND INSTALL ARDUINO ESP32 V1 DEVELOPMENT ENVIRONMENT

Now, if you have a board like the one that we have, which is E.S.P, first it will vote on one. You need to go to the tools and from the tools menu, you can simply go to the board, select parts manager, and from there. Right, E.S.P. Thirty-two now. If you didn't get any results, you need to do one thing before moving on. You need to add that E.S.P 32 Package Digest's on the file link to the preferences window. So let's go click file.

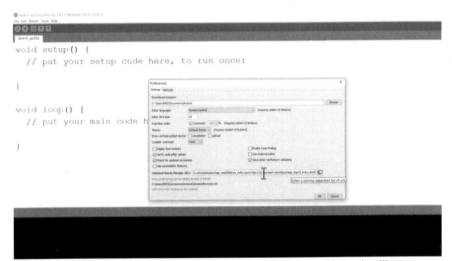

Preferences and here are the comma, then the second length. I'll give you all of these links in the resources project. Again, go to the tools board sports manager and here. Nuccitelli E.S.P. And here it is.

```
void setup() {
    // put your setup code here, to run once:

}

void loop() {
    // put your main code here, to run repeatedly:

}
```

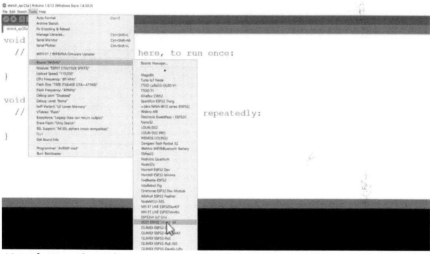

You can simply click install store. This Paul. It will take some time. Now, once you are done, you will see an assault here. Click loans and go to the tools menu. From there, you can check the ball. That's what you want to connect to and you can see that we have.

List of votes down here, you need to choose the one that matches your configuration. In our case. Okay, sorry. Now our case will be DeWit. E.S.P. And we need to choose to do it. E.S.P 32. So let's scroll up. OK, here we have E.S.P, 32 people, kit or AVL kit div module. And we have other E.S.P 32 modules, as you can see here. We need to do it. E.S.P. d'Hiv gets version one, which is the one that we have here and our labs. And we recommend it to everyone who is just getting started on the Internet of Things. So select it, then go. If you didn't see your ball. I have it on my OSPI bought. I have connected the board but I don't see a board here. In that case. You need to download and install this.

You must be to your art bridge driver. Now, not done that matches your operating system. Make sure to write this name. You are searching for it. If your board is E.S.P 32, depending on your board, there are other drivers. So click, download. Again. Click download here. Tech time, double click.

LOAD YOUR FIRST CODE TO THE ESP32 BOARD

Now, if you have everything connected correctly and if you went to the device manager,

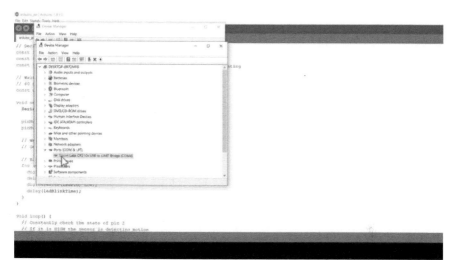

I did hook up my board so you should see your ball that comports in the name of the sea or silicone laps, which is that part of that was just an assault and the previous lesson. Now we know that our ball's connected to come forward. Let's head back to our software, make sure that you are choosing the right board.

Do it E.S.P 30 to defecate version one and go back again to select the ball. Choose Cornforth. Now, you can go to the examples and check some of the Wi-Fi examples. As you can see here, we have more than one.

You can check the Wi-Fi scan example. Now, this is a new sketch, as you can see, it's using a Wi-Fi library. You don't have to have any knowledge. All previous experience, to use this example or what you need to do now is simply flicked upload. Now it's combining the sketch and it's uploading that sketched-out E.S.P 30 to a bald. It usually takes some time since our Luigino isn't the native coding app for ESB want. As you can see, it's connecting using conformal. To. That E.S.P. Code. Now it's writing the code four percent. Hundred percent. Now it's hard sitting there. Yes. Board, as you can see from this menu, shows us all of the tables.

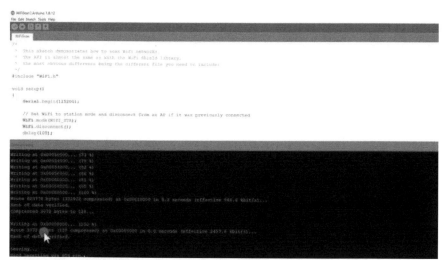

Again, that I think the process takes some time. Now, as you can see, done applauding. So go on, open up serial Molotov. Make sure that you have selected the right board rate, as you can see.

Now that the E.S.P board started the Wi-Fi scan and once it's done, it will show you the networks that are available in your area. I have these three networks, as you can see, one of them has a very weak signal. That's why it's coming and going. So this is my network. And this is someone's network. Now we have three networks. So. And this is a quote, an example of the Wi-Fi scan process. Next, we are going to dig deeper and start talking about how to test the lid on that board and how to control different elements using that port. Then we move on to the old page thing.

HELLO WORLD ON ESP32

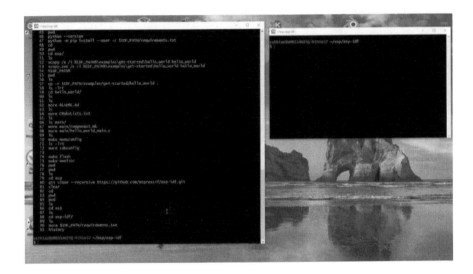

So now that you installed the audio IDC and then we installed the SPF I.D. let's make our first example in our SPF idea of the directory. So we opened my gateway the sorry the terminal by going to a directory maybe it installed my size 32 and we double click on men. It gave me 32, not EMC. And this opens up this terminal window. Now in this terminal window, we are here. N slash home city yes. And we had created an ESB directory here earlier from here we moved to its B IDF.

In this, we will see drink recall examples. That has all the examples that are provided to us to understand this code. So examples and we see we should see a hello world example here. Copy that and just give me a second word is the in the world here.

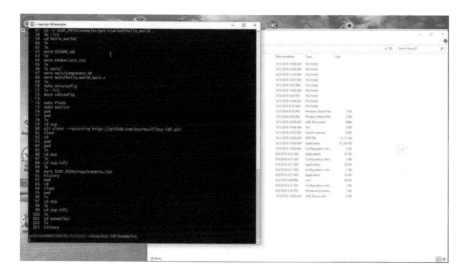

It's in examples get started. So to get started directory here and we see the hello world here. This one. So this is the directory gonna copy and runs this example program. So we go back to our home directory to ESB and here I'm going to make a copy of the hello-world directory.

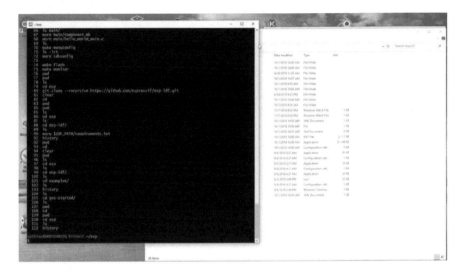

So I'll do a CPM minus r which is to copy this command that I had executed earlier which is here. Just copies the whole directory from the idea of that which is that from the ECB if the idea of bad examples gets started in the world and you copy it into this directory to not be done unless you see Hallowell here.

So this is how generally you write an application on ESB IDF if you move into this bakery you will see there is a component which is created under the main directory is a make file and then this does not like often files here going to mean and to see this one component call hello world underscore may not see and you have to have a mandatory firewall component to make it as empty if you open this file hello

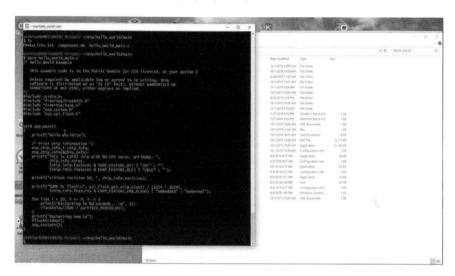

the world may not see it starts includes free to us preorders dot etch print some chip information and then so reboots in 10 seconds. So it's very simple to program and just shows you how to write a really basic program using ESB IDF. So now that you've made this program we go back and do the hello world mean rhetoric here and make a menu of why you're doing this.

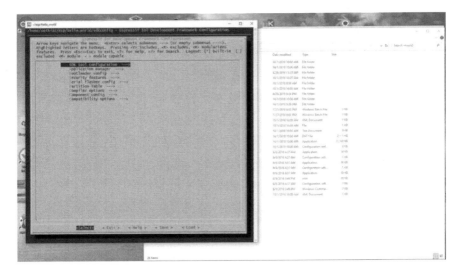

We should copy it.

We should also connect our ESB 32 hardware using the USP cable into our windows so that once we do that

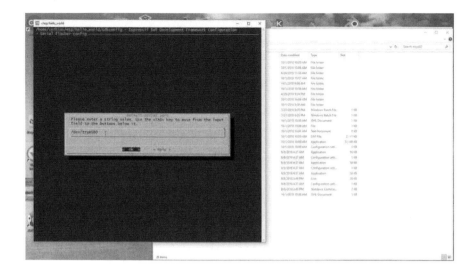

we can go into the senior flasher thing and change the possible port to whatever shows up in the Windows device manager. So let me just copy the USP into my laptop if this is connecting the ESB 32 OK. Once I do that I'm going to go into my device manager and see where the ESB 32 shows up.

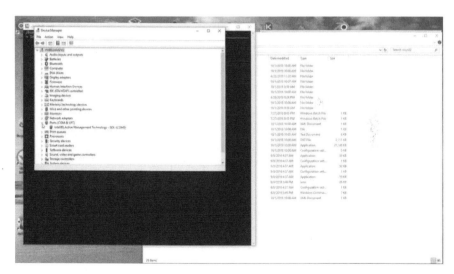

So I open this and I go to ports and it hasn't shown up all day default the deaths of people me to be here for a second will I find a port here.

HELLO WORLD ON ESP32 - PART2

So I have opened the device manager here and I installed the ECB 32 using the USP cable and I find that it comes up as come for in order we know that in the make menu conflict that we did in the last project we want to change that to come for and this is a Windows 10 I used here. So that's OK.

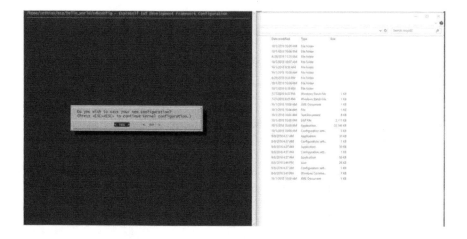

And that's all I want to do here for the hello world to exit this except this and save this configuration once I save this. It says that the next thing to do is to just do a make. And it will start compiling the application. So in the meantime, I'm going to open up another window by clicking on Main Gate 332 dot EMC and it will generate the config the SDK default on FAQs and all that once it is finished. Make Menu Config. Just go back to see what I did earlier. And I can just do a make flash and make money off of that.

So it is generating config to open other windows for us here so if I the directory here I mean ESB IDF to go back to a hundred tree in this that would do ESB directory and with an ESB.

This is what we have created the hello world and the make Menu Config is running here as you can see it's already started making these files the SDK is confident this decaying conflict at all and you can

open to config and you can see all the options just the way you see when you build it in

that system all the contradictions are here and you will see the com for port that we have set in this in this file here is that to come for a graphic for that as to get and there it is the conflict ESB tool by port because has been to the C program that is used to upload this sketch and it's going to look for this contradiction just to find out what component needs to use to send the sketch to ESB thirty two and that said to come forth so once this finishes once they make Menu Config finishes we're going to do a make flash which will basically compile the whole code I use the free are toss at the library and make one one package it will have the bin files and the partition information as well as the bootloader and we'll also upload this into the actual addresses on the ESB to reduce flash at the right places and it will start running the program OK and then for you to see the print deaths you can do a make monitor which opens up the monitor window and you can see all the printers coming on the make up on your window. So we want to do that now. Once this finishes here key the second more all these files here and wants to make menu content finishes aren't going to just do it make flash off of this so living bosses we do other it is it's done. My next step is making me Flash which will compile the whole program and link it with the free autos always another library that is using and we will make our binary file. Let us finish and then finally we'll do it will start running and we will make more order to see what the output of the hello world are coming up as let's see that.

HELLO WORLD ON ESP32 - PART3

So the make menu conflict completed and given the com for order number there for years be a tool to upload the code to b 32 and then I gave make flash so what the make flash did was compile everything including the Free orders and if you notice here it statically links our hello world program with the free order so everything becomes one compiled binary file and if you notice here then it invokes that ESPN will

not by and looks at both number com for and tries to connect to the SB 32 it's able to connect to it here and it say the chip number is this and starts uploading the binary file so that three binary file uploads in order here at 0 x 1000 is for K memory it uploads the bootloader at 0 extend thousand which is about thirty-two 2k it uploads the actual sketch and at eight thousand it applauds

the partition table so offered to upload the three binary files it goes and resets the is twenty-two and now it's and it only 2 is now instituting the hello world code on this window I have run make monitor someone deposit posit here will show you what's happening here again posted. If you go up to this point so let's say it starts from here you restart the ESB 32 here and at this point, you restarted it loads everything it boots up and from here these are print tests that are started coming in from 32. This is the system plaintext of the ESB IDF is loading second state bootloader has started and finally, the ESB Major is taken by looking at this partition table which has three partitions and another app is here which is the factory app and then it loads it and here it starts printing out us stuff that we had put in a global program can find that here it's cheap you start up brought the protocols use up the application use up the project name was hand a world that is what we had compiled as a component the compile-time and then then it gets other stuff here that we could look into I'm looking for stuff that we had printed and here it is 3D printing hello world and we're painting the chip information so this is a chip in E-Trade or chip but to see because with Wi-Fi Bluetooth silicon division one so on for megabyte flash and then we wait 10 seconds again restart.

So this is a simple high-level program that we compiled as a component of statically linked to all the free autos libraries and uploaded the sketch and then make monitor on this window to connect to the serial port of com for and see what the printers that are coming through. So great we got our whole program up we will write another program in the next project we'll get into more tried different APIs to the ESB idea gives up the act it gives us including increasing Wi-Fi Networking APIs and so on.

ESP32 STARTUP

So in this project, we see a bit more detail of how the helical application vote and how the ESB to the ordinary I.D. or the ESB IDF I.D. loaded the sketch that we had done into the SB 32. So going back to the global application we compiled it and we did make flash and then we saw a couple of these. So the second stowage second stage a boot loader then it printed out the partition table here.

This is the partition table which is saying that Yabulu rests a thousand your partition table your fact that the factory just compiled is at this address and the other various sort of labels given to the partition table and then it loaded the actual images here. Let may go down. It says the CPA was starting the protocol CPA was up and the project name is just not as Wi-Fi example is actually hello world. And the compile-time and then the ACBL starts coming up for some time here and then the protocols if you start the user code then both the CBO staff the scheduler. So let's start on the Protocols CBO and then the schedule starts on the app CBO said since we have two processors on this and three are also imported to run on these two processors the schedule runs on both the c bills OK. So let's see what's happening here now. So the ECB ready to start up the high-level view is as follows the first major first date bootloader in Rome Lord. The second stage bootloader emerged to ram into the flash from the flash offset 0 x 1000 which is better than reciting When we compiled an uproar. Let's get you to the flash. So from here when this area gets copied into the memory that's the second stage bootloader and that then loads of partition tables and the main app image from the flash the main app is what we have which is the actual quote free text-based application it incorporates both rhyme segments and it only segments. Matt why are the flash crash then the main app executes which is the two stages we saw. We were just looking at that like now which is the main app executing the protocol see you coming up the apps you coming up the be starting all that is happening from the main app. OK. So again First it bootloader resides in the wrong memory with a very small program. This we executed at each reset of the chip. It can fix the access to the external flash memory and if required stored it on new data coming from a single-use be put once finished it accesses the flash memory at zero thousand when you have the second stage it will color and it copies that into the ram and executes the continued load. The second stage bootloader reads the partition table directly eight thousand such as four patients. And maybe you copied the compiled sketch it decides which application has to be executed based on the contents of the audio data partition if this is empty or doesn't exist in our case it didn't exist we didn't have an audio data partition then we printed out the partition table we didn't have an audio data partition didn't exist because it doesn't exist it just it executes the fact the data is nothing but I was getting it just compiled. Okay, so this allows us to do the system which is the second stage bootloader to choose now. Victoria I'm sorry to choose which sketch it has to execute but it is a factory app but it is the next app that you uploaded over there. Do all the air out that you've got. You would have multiple partitions here. So this is what allows us to choose which application to load and run in the ESB 32 OK. So the second stage would put us in some more details in ESB IDF the binary made with the sites at 0 x 1000 in Flash is the second stage what I just mentioned this is the one that's copied into Ramadan exec and that get executed with a copy of the partition table and also copies the actual sketch into the ram. Second bootloader source code is available in components bootloader directly and then you're compiling you must have noticed that you're going to ask hello world here. People to build a rectory. You can put the bootloader. This is where you have not been filed which is copied into the 0 x 1000 location. This is your second-stage bootloader. So when the first gate bootloader load this boot would not have been filed and finish checking a log in the second it would order it jumps to the second stage would order entry point found in the binary image header. This second stage bootloader then reads the partition table founded off offset eight thousand which helps them decide which app to execute based on the various partitions that we have. And then what happens is that the second stage will go to configure the flash menu for both protocol and application CB use is a minor thing here that only enables the flash menu for the protocol. It doesn't do with the apps at this time primarily because the memory region that we're using right now is the way it is used by the app if cash so we cannot enable the enemy for the app's cache at this point. We do it later than once the code is loaded and the Flash menu is up seconds date bootloader jumps to the application entry point fine. Found in the binary image header, okay, and that entry point I just want to sort of move forward a bit. It is called the app's main function. If you notice every code will have an app main function.

Even if you went to the hello world of code. If you go to Hello one or two mean and you do well may not see this function is very important.

So this is the function that is is the function that the main task calls and is your app's main function. If this exists then the ready 32 it's over. I mean this is only cost as running on the free Tusk on the Fiat. Okay. Come back here. The ESB IDF application entry point is the be-all stock see below zero function found in this directory components is thirty-two you stop dot c two main things this function does enable the heap allocator and to make you jump to his entry point all you 1 but you have a false start CPR 0 and call start C.P. 1. These are the two entry points for the two processes that we have to call stock Cebu detail is the entry point for the CPO 0 and call starts if you want is the entry point for c v 1 now the code on the protocol you says the entry point for the ACP you d asserts the app will set and then only then the blue starts executing this function once it executes and it reaches a certain point then it sets a global flag which again indicates to the cold start see below zero that it can now proceed. So what these functions ultimately land up in something called start CPR 0 and start CPR 1. These two are vague functions that can be ordered but we won't go into those details right now but basically, these calls start CPR zero lands up into start see below zero which is running on the protocols if you and call start CPR one lands on start CPR one does running on the actual view both of these functions start the scheduler sees unlike your Linux or other operating systems where the scheduler started by the kernel here the scheduler is started here by but by these functions. So it is basically because the autos is a library that gets statically linked to your application and the whole thing becomes one big file. It's a bit different from the usual online program that you write in Windows operating system. So what the scheduler is started on the protocol. See you the apps. If you also start the scheduler and then very much your app main function gets called and your app takes over. So that is a very sort of quick high-level view of all the startup happens on iOS 32.

HELLO WORLD PROJECT STRUCTURE

Hi, folks welcome. So let's again look at the hello world program that we wrote of which is this function that has an

app main function that has been glued up included.

And if you look at the directory structure here you had the building that was made after it was compiled. There was a man which had the component and it had a make file and these were built after we had given the make of make flash command the conflicts. So essentially this as you can see some structure's being imposed when you want to write an application for free order. So we just go through that so that the design when you are working with the ESB IDF you have to write your application in a certain structure. So all the software applications that you write in the IDF the available components. The operating system the network stack by five drivers everything is a component to this design allows you to use your component app which is your application that you're writing or you can use third-party components as long as you follow the structure. So what is the structure? So this is a structure that has this main component. This is the primary component that has to exist and you could have a component directory that could have other components you could build a project which has many components the mandatory make file and then doesn't often instigate conflict or defaults it picks up the ticket configuration and a built like freeze made after you have compiled the code. This is exactly what we had seen here. Just look at it again. You know this. So I haven't the hello-world directory that has this means is the main component and has to make five mandatory pages. If you put it the main this has your component would make it just empty and Donnelly C programmers Hallowell Maine the North Sea and I bring this out. This has included fires and a mandatory at Maine which gets called by the yard up routines of yes. Because you do have to just sign the last project. So that's the sort of component application structure that you are you have to follow once you write an application for use.

EXAMPLE CODE

/* Hello World Example

This example code is in the Public Domain (or CC0 licensed, at your option.)

Unless required by applicable law or agreed to in writing, this software is distributed on an "AS IS" BASIS, WITHOUT WARRANTIES OR CONDITIONS OF ANY KIND, either express or implied.
*/

```c
#include <stdio.h>

#include "freertos/FreeRTOS.h"

#include "freertos/task.h"

#include "esp_system.h"

#include "esp_spi_flash.h"
void app_main()

{

  printf("Hello world!\n");
```

```
/* Print chip information */

esp_chip_info_t chip_info;

esp_chip_info(&chip_info);

printf("This is ESP32 chip with %d CPU cores, WiFi%s%s, ",

    chip_info.cores,

    (chip_info.features & CHIP_FEATURE_BT) ? "/BT" : "",

    (chip_info.features & CHIP_FEATURE_BLE) ? "/BLE" : "");
printf("silicon revision %d, ", chip_info.revision);
printf("%dMB %s flash\n", spi_flash_get_chip_size() / (1024 * 1024),

    (chip_info.features & CHIP_FEATURE_EMB_FLASH) ? "embedded" : "external");
for (int i = 10; i >= 0; i--) {
```

```
        printf("Restarting in %d seconds...\n", i);

        vTaskDelay(1000 / portTICK_PERIOD_MS);
    }

    printf("Restarting now.\n");

    fflush(stdout);

    esp_restart();

}
```

PROGRAMMING WITHOUT CODING SOFTWARE

What is visual before we start using the software, let's first understand what is the software and how it will make your life easier, which we know is a graphical integrated programming environment that helps use our program, microcontrollers, and microprocessors with the help of easy to use visual interface. It is a paid software, but it's available in a free version that you can use and you can simply download the free version by following the steps that we have in the next section, which is more than enough to get started using this software and to reduce the programming complexity for beginners, with which we know you can create a wide variety of projects. And it supports all the popular boards like Arduino Raspberry Pi E.S.P and its compatible boards. It also supports the E.S.P series. And even as species like Raspberry Pi, which we already mentioned, with this software in hand, you can easily code anything without writing a single letter. You just need to drag and drop components in the visual interface, as you can see in this image. And your software and the software will take care of the coding and will convert your drawing into a text file that you can upload to a microcontroller. So I think that it's a very good software for beginners and for anyone who hates programming or wants to create software on the goal without going on the headache of programming and coding or writing a lot of lines. Again, if you are just getting started or if you have a kid, you can teach him how to program using the software.

DOWNLOAD AND INSTALL PROGRAMMING SOFTWARE

I'm going to teach you how to download and install the software that we are going to use to program the board without coding. Now, the software.

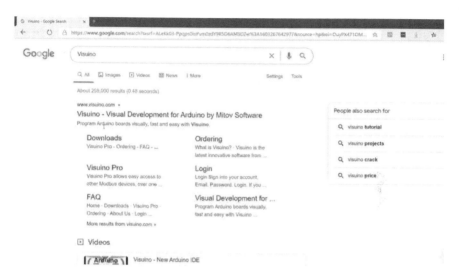

It's called visual, so light, visual, and as you can see is the first result click downloads.

 And from here you can see that this software comes in two versions, a free version that you can use and you can easily do whatever you want with. But it has some limitations. And as a starter, I don't think that you need a bad version. So let's get started. This is a list of the improvements inside this version of the software, which is the latest version. As you can see, they have improved the DH to 11 cents or support and counters array's text memory, LCD modules, and a lot of other stuff. So click here to download that software. It shouldn't take long, as you can see, it's about one hundred thirty-one megabytes, so it should take a minute or two to download. Now, let's take a quick look at their website. As you can see, they are working to add download profile pages for the vision approval and they have approved Virgin Vision approval. As you can see here, you can order their version. But again, I don't think that it's necessary. You can use the free version to program any board that you have. And this is the list of the supported boards, Arduino Boards Raspier by Tensei from 2R I all E.S.P 32 on DSP 80 to 66 and control, you know, and among other boards. There is also support for Arduino clones, the boards that you make at home and look the same as Arduino. And this is the user interface. Now. I mean, it left for the download. As you can see now, the downloads finished 100 to one megabyte. Just open the file and you can extract it or you can simply double click on the setup, that file. Now, this is the download.

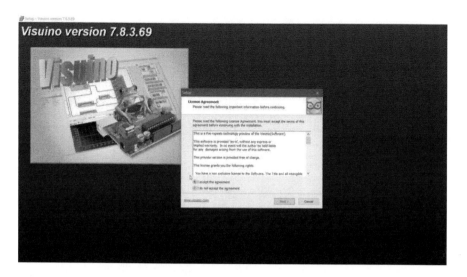

Or the installation wasn't clicked, I accept the next, next, then install. Now, once the installation process is over, as you can see, Saddam has finished installing visual version seven point eight on your computer, just click finish and it will launch the software. So finish. It will take some time to load the libraries depending on your computer hardware. As you can see, this is the user interface and we are going to introduce everything inside this user interface and the coming lessons. But if you did reach this step, it means that you have the software and it's fully functional.

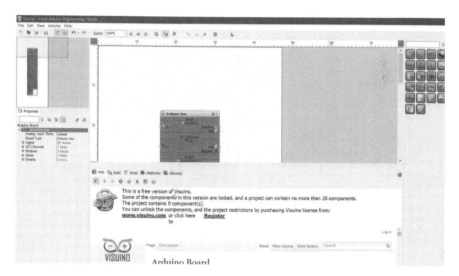

You need to take this not into consideration. This is a free version of, you know, some of the components in this version, and this version are locked. And a project can contain no more than 20 components, which is more than enough for us since we are just getting started with this. Now, if you want the full features, you have to go and buy the software. But again, I don't think that you need to buy it for any components is more than enough.

DOWNLOAD AND INSTALL ARDUINO IDE

First, you must go and search for Arduino I.D. using Google or Bing. The first is that Windows, you see, which is the official Arduino website.

You can either use Darwin Web editor without installing software or you can download the Arduino ID now, depending on your operating system, you must choose one of these Windows, Mac, or Linux for my case, its Windows installer. Now it's asking you to donate or you can just download. Click on Save. And you have to wait about three minutes for the download to finish. Now let's see the Arduino website. It offers. A lot of products. As you can see here. You can share any of these items from the official website. These items include Arduino boards. Green kids and a lot of other interesting stuff. Now let's see the other kids category. As you can see, this kid, um, this is all about kids. It has a very. OK. A very interesting collection. You can also buy Arduino boards or windshields. Let's look at boards and modules and see how much each of these boards might cost you. This is the official place to buy Arduino boards. You need to make sure that you are not buying from places that offer a fake ALGUIEN on boards or boards that are not manufactured, bought by the original company. OK. The export of arms to. Can also check the learning section for tutorials, reference and things on new things to learn. As you can see here, the boards, the entry-level have only Leonardo and starter kit. No, no mini micro.

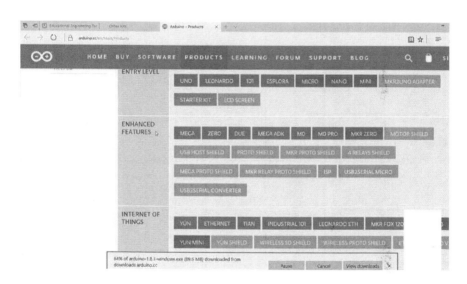

The enhanced feature has the Amiga, the Internet of Things has others. As, yes, I'm sheild the proposals for making, let's say, a smartwatch, the printing section for making a 3D printer. Let's see the Ormeau. And the mega. This is, uh. Arduino material one zero one, a symbol 3D printer, as you can see. Looks. Mines will cost you around 700 hundred dollars. You can also see the arguin on board. It'll cost you 25, 24 dollars. Twenty-five dollars. Aldwin, onum. As you can see, this is the original stuff. Now, to move your borders or not, you can flip it if it's a symbol in the USA or

Germany, then it's original. The ones that are assembled in China are not created by the official Arduino company. It's created by Arduino associates. And it must cost less about ten to twelve dollars or debauches such bolds. They are not there don't have the same quality as the ones manufactured in the A.

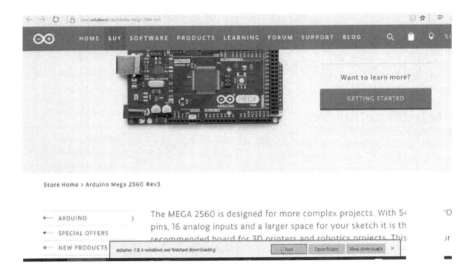

OK, now let's see the Arduino finished downloading, let's run a download Arduino has already installed, so you have to understand the one that you have. OK, let me see. You have to close an instance, you know, all of that, you have opened, then uninstall. The previous version. As you can see, it's removing the files. If you already have Arduino and installed your computer, you need to update it with the latest version if you already have the largest version and then please skip this one, click on next install, as you can see, the installation or started.

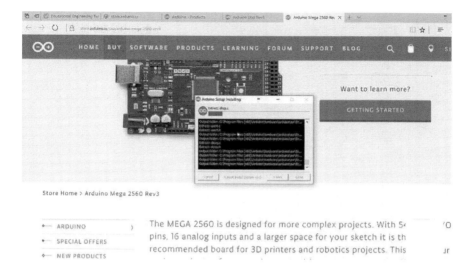

It won't take long. You can check out the section, the scores to download the code, and the material to get links for the hardware material. OK. OK, and I had to close then go to the start menu. Go to the Eleazar, then choose Alino. This is our man Padrino ideating. Now, to make a quick overview, this is the button that you must click to verify that your code is written correctly. This one is used to verify and upload Dakotah Arduino. These are for orbit and save this to create a new file. As you can see, when you create a new file, you have two main methods the setup and loop the setup for your setup code. The loop is for your code that will run repeatedly. And the fine is common sense, Skitch is used to upload, verify the code or add new libraries. The tools as used to choose the ball, should the board give the ball, inform, choose the programmer Bernard Bootloader, which is an advanced topic, and Arduino opens the serial monitor or serial Bl?? tter, fix the encoding of the code or the format. It help is where you can find, uh, things. You are looking for its answers.

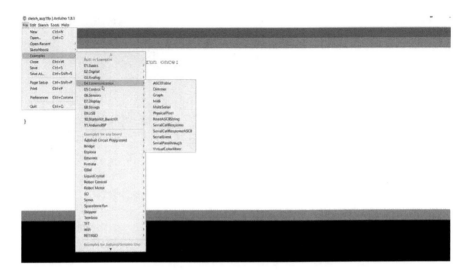

Now you can check examples, basic digital analog communication controls, and sort of display. Let's see that we want a basic example for blinking led, as you can see, this is a blinking led example. It's very simple, straightforward it's commented so that you can understand what's happening and what's going on. So that's why Arduino is very. Popular because it would provide amazing support. That's it for this lesson, if you have any questions, please ask. And if you want Ebor,

DOWNLOAD AND INSTALL ARDUINO ESP AND USB DRIVER

Now, let's get started with software set up, hang onto your keyboard and mouse. This part might get bumpy follow along closely as we configure and upload our first day, Iwai wi-fi connected software. And this lesson will install the E.S.P eight two six six Balde package inside our Arduino software. We will also install a device driver for the board communication chip and upload an Arduino sketch that connects to your home wireless network. The good news is that once you have completed the steps and this and this lesson, you won't have to do them again. You are using the same computer and the same ball, you don't have to reconfigure and reinstall any of the software that we are going to install and the software or in this lesson. So the first step will be installing the Arduino software. As you already know, the hardware-software is available for free on the Arduino, the Cissie website. So the first step will be going to the Arduino, the Cissie go to the software section, click downloads. And from here, choose your operating system, in our case, it's Windows operating system, we can use the Windows installer, all the windows up, and I already installed the windows up. Here it is.

```
char serialData;
int pin = 13;

void setup() {
  // put your setup code here, to run once:
  pinMode(pin, OUTPUT);
  Serial.begin(9600);
}

void loop() {
  // put your main code here, to run repeatedly:
  if (Serial.available() > 0)
```

Now, by default, the Arduino application support chips used an official Arduino board, but not the E.S.P board. These boards can be programmed out of the box because the Arduino application already knows about each one and its properties. One cool thing about Arduino is that you can add support for other bolts and all you have to do is to tell and we know where to discover their priorities. The first step of that process is providing you can the additional board's manager. Now. You have to go to the edit, and from there you need to go to the File menu and select preferences, you will get to see this window. As you can see here, we have an additional boards manager. You are adults and you have to based specific. You are all in that window. I will give it the resources of this project, but here it is. Let me copy and paste that you are on.

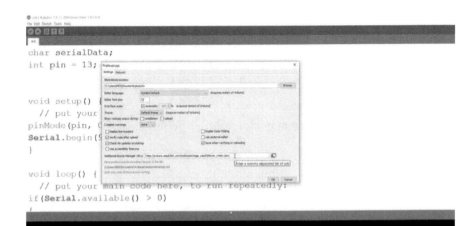

This is the original E.S.P, you are all for this package. Now, if the box was not blank where you opened the preferences window, you may have some other boards already installed. If that's the case, I that Xbox contact with the above, we are all using a comma to separate different Yahel. So you can add this one and add a comma and add another one. But since we only have one, I will base it here after doing that. Click OK to play to close that preferences window. Now our original application knows where to find info about the sport in general. So let's go to the tools. And from there. Go to the board's manager. And here and the boss manager, you need to write E.S.P. Now, as you can see here, we have E.S.P. Eight two six-six, what you need to do is simply click install. It will take some time to download about 34 megabytes of data to your Arduino libraries folder, and once done, it will show you a message indicating that everything is done. Now, once it's done, as you can see, it says installed here, you can click close. And if you want to the board manager, you can see that now we have E.S.P eight two, six, six and E.S.P eight to eight-five and other E.S.P balls.

Most of them are here now, what you need to do is simply start using them and I already mentioned that the one that we have. At hand is the E.S.P fair to the eight to six six million now? To make sure that it's recognized when connecting the USB port, you need to install any additional driver from the Sealab website. I will give you links to this driver as well. So you need to go and check your operating system. And we have IndusInd Universal. So we will use this software, click download VCP.

The download will start, you can simply click download, after that you can install. The driver, depending on your operating system, that's it. Now, we have installed the hardware-software that E.S.P library for Arduino and the USB drive driver.

ESP 32 PINOUT V1 DOIT

Hello and welcome to the stimulus on Energy are going to talk about E.S.P 30 to open out, which are purpose input-output pens, should you use now?

This is how the physical layout of that E.S.P board locks and as you can see, it's very similar to the Arduino Nano, but it has a Wi-Fi built and now they are speed first to peripherals, include 18 digital converters or ADC channel, where you can receive analog signals and these signals can be converted to digital internally. It also has three S.P.I interface for communication and three, your art interfaces for communication and to all to see interfaces for Seattle communication. So these, let's say, eight modules or light pens can be used to allow cell communication with multiple devices that support S.P.I eye to see or eyes accuracy and your art. It also has 16 PWI output channels which help produce an analog output from the expense. It also has two digital channel converters and two eye-to-US interfaces. It also has 10 capacitive sensings, special-purpose input-output. I provide more data and more details about each of these pens in the resources project, but since we have a lot of them, we don't want to get caught in the details. Now, what we need to know is that pan out itself. As you can see, this is how the board looks.

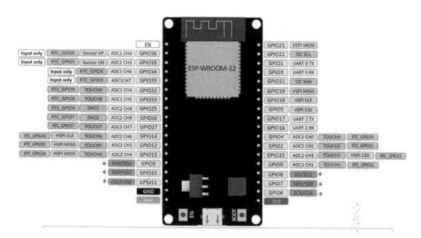

This is the USPI board and you are going to hook up your Glaspie Connector here and the other side will be connected to your computer. As you can see, these are the pens, g.p. I mean, the real purpose, input-output. Now, there is more than one general-purpose, input-output, as you can see here. And each of these pens has more than one function. As you can see, usually Bend's comes with many names such as PII and ADC and Digital Converter and General-Purpose and put out so you can use it as an input-output pen or receive an analog signal or for S.P.I or for all to see. So the choice is yours now, as you can see, these pens, all of them are numbered for easy access so that you can easily know which pen is connected to each. Now, additionally, there are pens with specific features that make them suitable or not for a specific project. The following demonstration shows you some of these pens. And I'm going to talk about each of these pens in detail and if they can be used as input or output.

GPIO	Input	Output	Notes
0	pulled up	OK	outputs PWM signal at boot
1	TX pin	OK	debug output at boot
2	OK	OK	connected to on-board LED
3		RX pin	HIGH at boot
4	OK	OK	
5	OK	OK	outputs PWM signal at boot
6	X	X	connected to the integrated SPI flash
7	X	X	connected to the integrated SPI flash
8	X	X	connected to the integrated SPI flash
9	X	X	connected to the integrated SPI flash
10	X	X	connected to the integrated SPI flash
11	X	X	connected to the integrated SPI flash
12		OK	boot fail if pulled high
13	OK	OK	
14	OK	OK	outputs PWM signal at boot
15	OK	OK	outputs PWM signal at boot
16	OK	OK	

Now, the pens are highlighted in green here. I'll show you a table to summarize this information. Again, the pins highlighted in green are OK to use the ones highlighted in yellow are OK to use, but you need to pay attention because they may have unexpected behavior, mainly at both times, while the pins highlighted in red are not recommended to use as input or output. Now, that general-purpose input-output PIN zero is, as you can see, OK to use. But you need to pay extra attention because it may have unexpected behavior at both times so it can be used as a pull-up input or as output. It outputs signal output, but no one can be used as ti expen for communication or output when it debugs output. Number two is OK to be used as input or output and usually, it is connected to unboarded so you can use it to test a code or to test our basic function because you don't have to connect extra components at all that you have built and led to. Number three is OK to use as input, but you can't use it as output. It's high output. So it will read one output. Ben, numbers four and five are OK to use as input to output, and PIN five also output SPW and signal output pins from six to 11 are connected to the integrated S.P.I Flash. So you can't use them as input or output. But No.12 is OK to use, but both will fail if Bould High, so it's OK to use as input. But you need to pay extra attention to this not. And if you are connecting it as output, it's OK. You don't have any problems. Pins from 13 to 16 are OK to be used as input or output without paying extra attention. Now as you can see, the same fourpence from 17 to 33, while 34, 35, 36, and 39 are input only pense you can't, you can't use them as output. Now, on our examples and our practice tests, we are going to use PIN two, which has built and laid on board, built and led and using that on board, built and led will make it easier for us to test out or to try different things if we are making Auberge with a baton to control it via the Internet. Now that's it for the pinout. Now I will add extra information, uh, So let you know more information about the general-purpose input-output bins. But for me, what I need you to know at this point is that we have bins that can be used easily without any extra attention as input-output, which are dispensed to four, five, 13 to 16, and 17 to thirty-three. And if we want to input only bins, we can use 34, 35, 36, or 39. Now, if we need extra features, if we need B.W., um, ADC or DSE, if we need a capacitor enabled bin or BW, and then we can go on and check this schematic. And from these bins, you can see that in our case, sharp elbows PIN thirty-six can be used as ADC or Douceur converter. As you can see, and it has the only state, you can use this schematic printed out to refer to it whenever you need to do something. Same for here. You can see from this image that PIN 25 can be used as a digital to analog converter and PIN 26 can also be used as the central converter or digital converter. So depending on what you need or what's your end goal, you are going to check this schematic and make sure that you choose the pin that fits your needs. So if you are going to use a pin as an output, you can't use PIN 34 because as you can see here, it's only input, only PIN. And if you want to use, let's say, analog to digital converter, you can't use this pin PIN 17 because it only supports zero communication and input-output, a regular input-output or digital input-output. So before using any pin, uh, take a minute or two to make sure that it supports what you are going to do and the sensors or the stuff that you are going to connect it to, and whether they are analog or digital, they are input like pushbutton or output like LEDs You need to connect the element to the right pin before start coding to avoid having problems in the future. Once you start testing your code.

WHAT IS THE ESP32 BOARD

SB 32 Development Board. The SB 32 is a low-cost system-on-chip series created by its price systems. It's an improvement on the popular E.S.P eight two six six that is widely used on Internet of thing products. The SB 32 has both Wi-Fi and Bluetooth capabilities, which make it an all-rounder chip for the development of Internet of Things Project and Embedded Systems Engineer. Now, in this project, you will learn how to get started with that E.S.P 32 and learn how to use it to scan Wi-Fi hotspots, control LEDs, batons, sensors, or get sensors reading on our page along with other examples. This project will equip you with the basic knowledge that you'll need when working on your ESB 32 projects in the future. Now, some of the main specifications for the E.S.P 32, when it comes to the CHIP specifications, you will find that it has a dual-core, which means that it has two processors. It also has Wi-Fi and Bluetooth built. And you don't have to plug in any you us b dongle to enable Wi-Fi or get a module. It runs 32-bit programs. The clock frequency can go up to 240 megahertz and it has 512 kilobytes from this particular board has 30 or 36 spins, 15 in each row. It also has a wide variety of peripherals available, like capacitive touch sensors and a digital converter digital-analog converter Universelle, synchronous Syria communication modules as P I, I squared C, and much more. This board comes with built-in hall effects and saw and built and temperature sensors. So this board is all that you need to get started. In no time in the Internet of Things. Now to start programming this board, you'll need software or a programming environment. You can simply use the added window idea, which we are going to do in discourse. It's very easy to use software and most people are familiar with it. And if even if you are not familiar, it's the easiest software to use when you want to program E.S.P bonds. There is also software as plosive IDF software. It's an interactive thing, a development framework that they provide for their boards. There is also Micro Python, JavaScript, or LUA. The one that we are going to use in this project is our idea. It requires some adjustments to install the E.S.P library, but everything will be explained in detail in a separate section where you will learn how to download and install the required libraries for different E.S.P boards and the right steps to do so. Now to prepare your board. For the Arduino, Ali, the E! There is an add-on for the Arduino I.D. that allows you to program the E.S.P thought to use that platform, the very same platform that you can use to program Arduino can also be used to program E.S.P. Using Arduino programming language. So it's out of the box and ready for you to use and in the next lesson, we are going to explain that E.S.P set to pinout how many pins are there, how to recognize each pin function, and which pin to use when you want to connect input-output. B.W. signal or sensor.

DOWNLOAD AND INSTALL ARDUINO ESP32 V1 DEVELOPMENT ENVIRONMENT

And know if you have a board like the one that we have, which is E.S.P 32 version one,

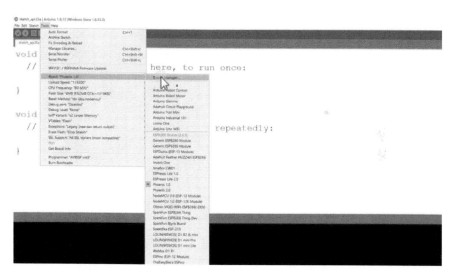

you need to go to the tools and from the tools menu, you can simply go to the board, select parts manager, and from the right E.S.P.

```
void setup() {
  // put your setup code here, to run once:

}

void loop() {
  // put your main code
}
```

Thirty-two now. If you didn't get any results, you need to do one thing before moving on, you need to add that SB 32 package digest on the file link to the preferences window. So let's go click file. Preferences and here are the comma, then the second length. I'll give you all of these links in the resources project again, go to the tools board sports manager and here. Kukali E.S.P. And here it is, you can simply click install to install this, Paul. It will take some time. Now, once you are done, you will see installed here, click close and go to the tools menu. From there, you can check the board that you want to connect to and you can see that we have. A list of balls down here, you need to choose the one that matches your configuration in our case. OK, sorry. In our case, it will be it. E.S.P, and

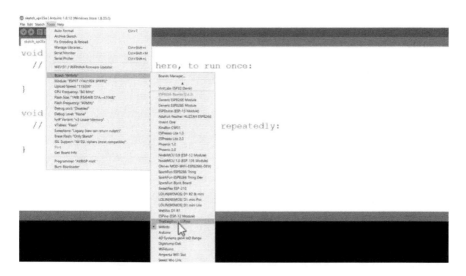

we need to choose the SB 32, so let's scroll up. OK, here we have E.S.P, 32 people get ready for this module and we have other E.S.P 32 modules, as you can see here. We need that word E.S.P to get version one, which is the one that we have here and our labs. And we recommend it to everyone who is just getting started on the Internet of Things. So select it, then go if you didn't see your ball. I have it on my OSPI board, I have connected the ball, but I don't see a board here in that case. You need to download and install this and your USB to your art bridge driver now, not the one that matches your operating system. Make sure to write this name when you are searching for it if your board is E.S.P 32, depending on your board. There are other drivers. So click, download. Again. Click download here won't take time, DoubleClick.

USER INTERFACE

Regino user interface, now the software user interface is straightforward, it's very simple, let's go and open up the software, Vilarino.

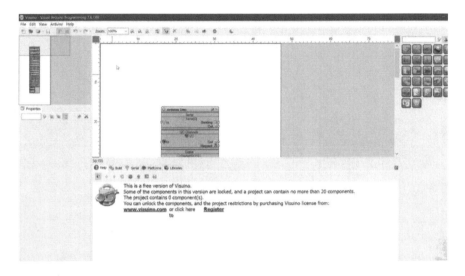

Now, as you can see in the center, we have the main block, which represents the actual microcontroller, and in this case, we have Arduino horno as the default microcontroller.

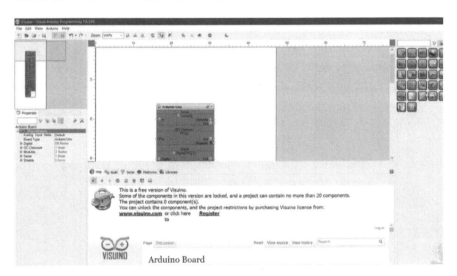

We can change this to any other microcontroller and you can scroll and this main block using this scroll and the right side, or you can simply drag and drop using this window, using your left mouse click. OK, now, dragging and dropping is usually to get inside and see all the pins in your microcontroller. As you can see, we have digital-analog pens, output, and input. So to see all of them, we need to scroll. So depending on how many pins your microcontroller might have, you might need to scroll a little bit longer. Now, on the right side, we find all components blocks like math, logic, digital, analog, and so on. As you can see here, we have the math. Here we have the measurement, memory, motors, generators, input-output, the integers, the stacks, seats, radio, and a lot of others. As you can see, we have coloring remote controllers. So it has a lot of tools that you can use for simulation and programming. Now, on the left side, we can edit the properties of the selected component, so we have the Arduino on selected. You can see here that we have the properties for this board, which is the Arduino.

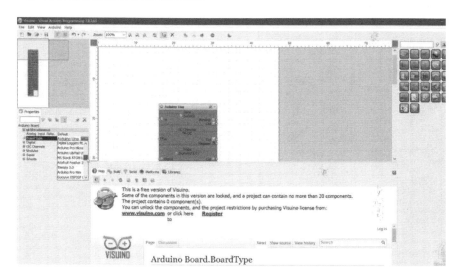

Now, you can click here and change the board type with any other board like E.S.P or another Arduino board. As you can see here, we have SB 32. And you have to give it some time to load the new board, and this is on your board. So from this one, you can change the probabilities for each of the components that you have. Now, let's try and add any component like this one.

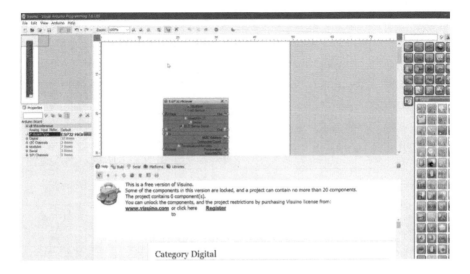

Category Digital

As you can see, this component, once you click on it, you can simply see that you have the component properties and name right here on the left side and you can play with it. You can easily select the ball by clicking this. As you can see this icon.

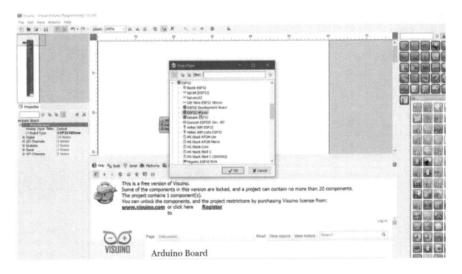

Arduino Board

And here you can search for the ball type. You can search for any of the balls. Yes, 32. And you will get a list of sports, as you can see that this the software supports. And here is one of them. And you can change the ball from this menu here on the left. Now, in the next lesson, we are going to start adding components together and we are going to design a simple circuit and connect it to start programming again. There is no coding required here. You just need to drag and drop. Stay tuned.

USER INTERFACE IN DETAILS

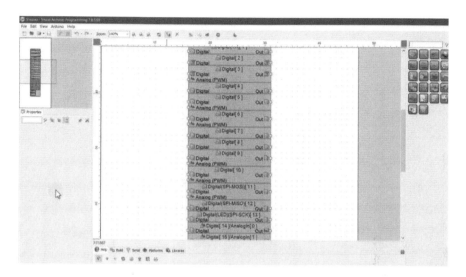

Now, let's talk about the visual user interface. We want to discuss the main components, the Left-Right and the canvas area, as you can see here, we have on our menu the file menu. You are already familiar with most of the items here. You open safe as reopen print and print it up, plus the exit.

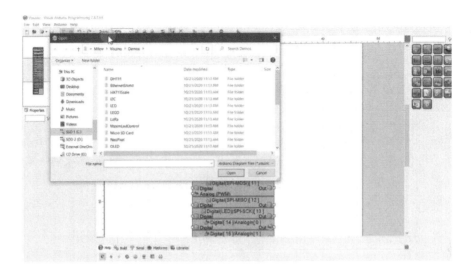

Now we have that open demo menu, which you can use to open examples that are already there, as you can see, is out for examples right here, like the middle class, the card also the example using the square, see all example. And we have the TV out. We controller a lot of very useful examples that are also on our list, for example.

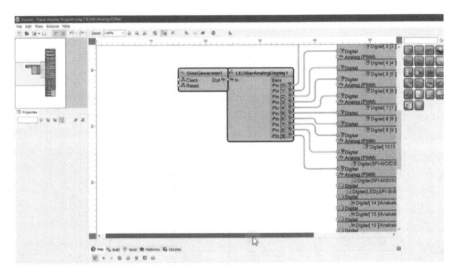

And once you open up any of these examples, you can see it and scroll to see how it's coded, as you can see in this. Now, the edit is also a very. Come on the menu, you can order a route using this menu route if I wait for the software that can roll the White House itself using automation and we have a copy as a picture. You can copy the whole thing as a picture. And if you went to the pen software. Inside your windows, you can paste that picture right here or you can paste it in the chat message for your friends and messenger WhatsApp or any other chatting software. And we have the hard copy and paste options and the already familiar with these. We have the undo underdo to undo changes and redo them. We have arranged for filters. We can select all components.

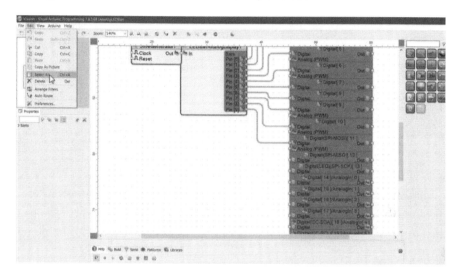

You are using the edit select all on by clicking control we can delete everything in here, as you can see by simply clicking delete. But the microcontroller will stay since it's the core of this project now we can undo the delete process by clicking that undoes. Now you can change the software preferences from this menu right here.

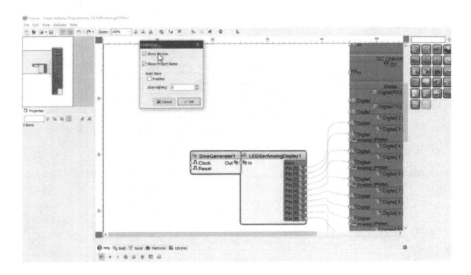

As you can see, you can choose to show the version or not. This is the version you can choose to show the project name or not. You can enable the autosave feature. And I do recommend enabling this feature and minimizing this to one minute because most of the time we forget to save our work and it's gone. So enabling the autosave feature is a very important thing. Click OK, now the version is gone and will autosave every minute.

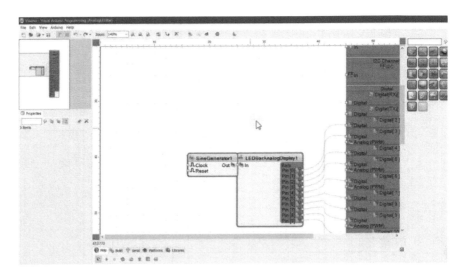

Going to your as you can see, these dots are called grid, so if you click here, they are gone, and usually, you can use them to aid, uh, with your connection to place components. On this grid, as you can see, as a moving and moving and these points, I don't move freely. And if you like to move freely on your canvas, you can deselect them and as you can see, you can move whatever you want. But I always like to keep them on. Now, the rules are the dimensions here on the canvas. So if you clicked here, they are gone. If you clicked again, they will show up. You can also check the dark theme.

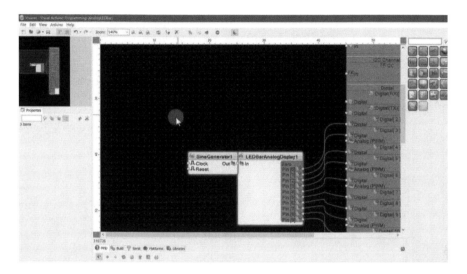

It has a dark theme if you are working at night or if you don't like the light color on your screen, you can change to the dark theme. Then we have the board properties, since we have our board, we have Arduino here, you can build your code, you can send it to the original idea as a code.

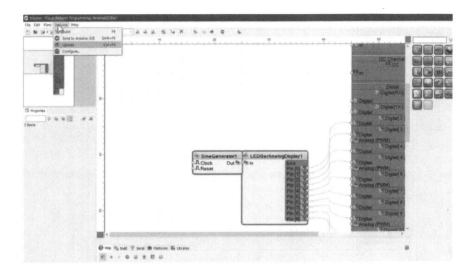

You can upload it, as you can see, by clicking here. But you have. To select the right path. OK, let me drag this up here.

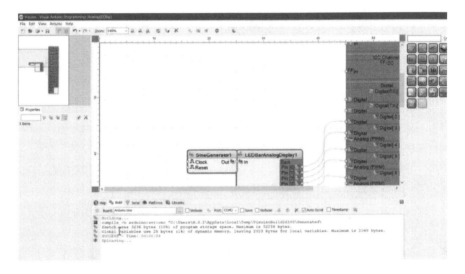

As you can see now, it's uploading the code directly to our Arduino board without going to the Arduino I.D. software. But as you can see, the composite selected is the one composite we have to select Comm Port four for the Arduino and make sure that the right Arduino board name is selected here. It will take a few seconds to upload. I usually prefer to upload using the Arduino I.D. software, but you can use this shortcut.

Now, there is also the Conficker, and as you can see in the configuration, you can select the location of the original idea.

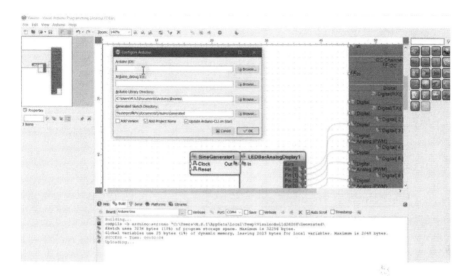

If you already have installed it, you can leave it by default. You can select the abdominal library directory and it's already here by a default setting for the search directory. And I'll do the idea. These are selected by default. So you don't need to change anything in here. Go back and select build. After that click upload, now I have the original owner board and Acom for selected, so it shouldn't take a lot of time to upload the code.

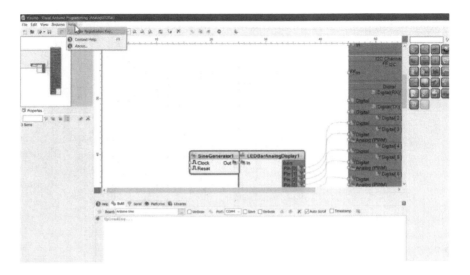

Now, that is the help menu, if you have a key, you can't simply enter it here, you can use the help section or see the software version as you can see their website, the logo, and click, OK.

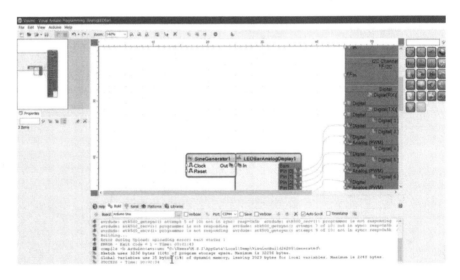

Now, this is regarding the main menu. OK, as you can see, success now. It did upload the code to our Arduino. OK, now let's go to this menu that has the very same things that are available here, but an icon mode, you can enable or disable the grid. You can enable or disable the ruler, redo and undo and redo. You can zoom in and out, as you can see in your design. Up to 10 percent. Now you can zoom in and out. By a margin of 10 using these icons, or you can.

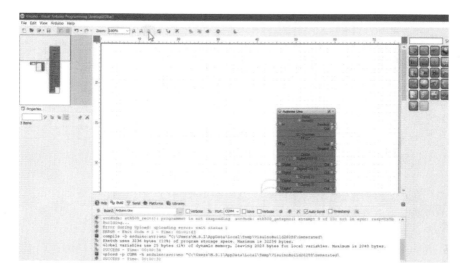

Return to 100 percent canvases using this icon. Now we have the save option and we have the open demo feature that opens examples that you can use to open examples. And we have that new project icon. Moving forward, we have the outer range. And this orange feature is a way for the software to arrange the items on your canvas. Now, if you have them, let's say not arranged. Let's say this one is here and you don't feel that this is the best arrangement.

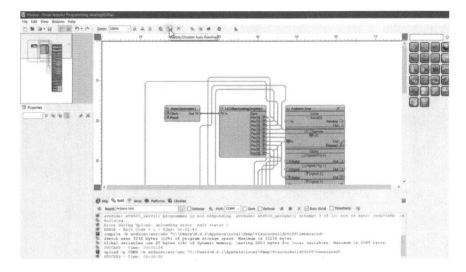

You can click once here and you'll find the best way and rearrange the items now to enable and disable the looting.

As you can see, that auto-routing feature is a way for the software to find the best route for the components to be connected. And as you can see, that whole thing did change when we clicked on the other routing. Now you can go back to the old rooting. This is the old routine, and once you click here, it will alter and change the routine. Now, as you can see here, you can delete the selection.

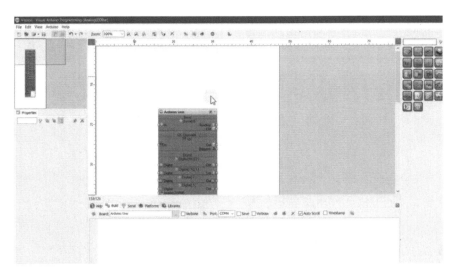

And by the latest selection, we have deleted everything that was selected. So let's go back and OK, these are all right. Now, here we have the Arduino menu items, the build to build your code or combine it. If you want to open the folder, you can open it up here.

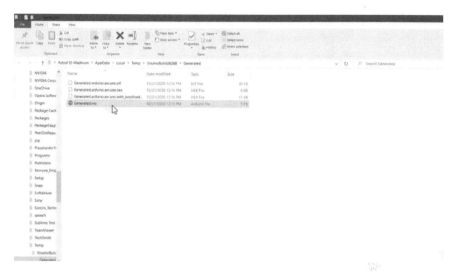

Here we have the hex file and here we have the Arduino Ono file. And what is usually uploaded is the text file to your Arduino. Now, here we have the upload to Arduino directly from this software. And here we can use this icon to send the code to our Arduino I.D. software. And this is to enable and disable the d'Harcourt. We already explained this menu and this menu and the probabilities menu. Now, let's take a quick look at the lower menu. In the battle here, we have the help section and as you can see, they have different tutorials here. We have the build section where you can choose the board that comports save auto-scroll and uploads your code. You will see the results here. Here we have the serial communication. If you want to send serial data to Arduino or to receive serial data from Arduino, you can simply select the homeport and click connect here.

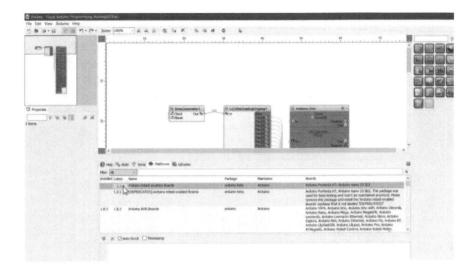

Now, here we have the platforms that the software supports, as you can see, that are updatable not installed or installed, you can install all of these depending on your needs and how much space you have. Here we have the libraries that this software supports, Bluetooth libraries, also libraries, touchscreen libraries, and other stuff, you can simply double click and all of these libraries to check the version, as you can see here. That's it. This is everything you need to know about the user interface.

EXAMPLE BLINK LED WITH ONE CLICK

we are going to start using E.S.P first to board and cording it,

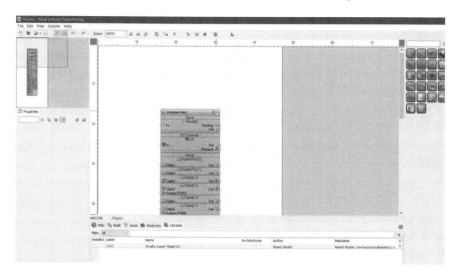

using drawing without basically lighting any called. So to get started, you need to open up the software if you haven't already got a start menu and click vaginal. Now, we already explained how to change the board, so go here and click select board.

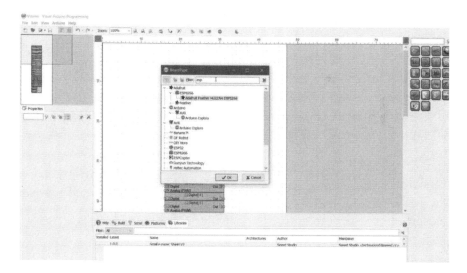

And from here, you have E.S.P 32. As you can see, we have various people, 32 here under the banana pie tag and we have an ISP filter to tag. As you can see, under this time, we have a lot of balls and you can pick any of these balls depending on the one that you have, all the modules that you are using. Now, for the sake of this lesson, we will select General E.S.P 32 and click on it. Now, as you can see, this is the E.S.P 32 ball, and as you go, you can see that it has serial square sea channels, digital channels, and was input-output and they are number up to 39. And we have to spy channels.

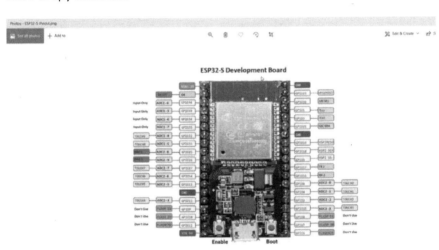

Now, if you are not familiar with that E.S.P 32 development board, this is how it looks and it has an all-purpose, purpose, and what output pens are numbered, as you can see here. Plus it has dual function pens. As you can see. These are inputs, only pens, and they support the conversion. These are for flashing, these are digital converters. These are for server communication and this is the square quercetin. It's also general-purpose input-output, PIN twenty-one now, and our software here. We have the digital section, as you can see, input-output separated from the square C section and it's separated from the ASPEY channels, but these are most likely intersected because as you can see here in this image, we don't have a pen that has the name Aspey Eye or I Squirty. We have a PIN. So General-Purpose Input-Output PIN twenty one supports our square. See, it's that as the Abin and General Purpose Input Output PIN twenty-two is the square see as Sculpin. So again these pins have dual functions. Button our visual software, they are separated so that you can easily recognize them. Now as you can see, what we are going to start with is the digital general-purpose input-output pens. Now, go to that component, many on the right side, and look for a pulse. Generator. As you can see here, we have a pulse generator and placed it right here. Go up usually general-purpose and put out the PIN two has an internal lid, so to turn on this internal ID, we need to connect the output of the pulse generator to the digital input of the spin.

Now, even if it doesn't have an internal lead, you can connect 20 to 120 resistors and led to this spin using your hardware set up and it will turn on and off. Now, as you can see here, the frequency is one, so it will turn on and off with a frequency of one hertz. You can change it from here. And this is basically how you can do the blink example on your ISP 32 baud.

UPLOAD BLINK LED CODE AND TEST IT

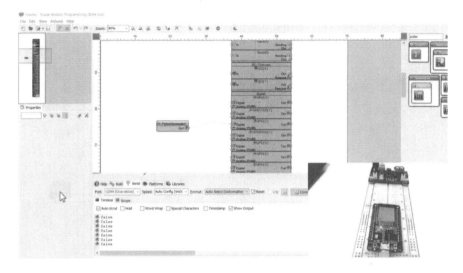

I'm going to show you how you can easily upload this code to your ISP, but now they ask people that we have here is the ISP 32 dev kit version one. So. This code will turn on and off at a frequency of one hertz using this Pulcinella through, which is connected to general-purpose input-output PINtwo. And this spin has an internal lid, which is the Brulard that will blink once we applaud the code. Now click on the Arduino icon. You must collect your ISP board and go to the device manager by clicking here on the start menu device manager.

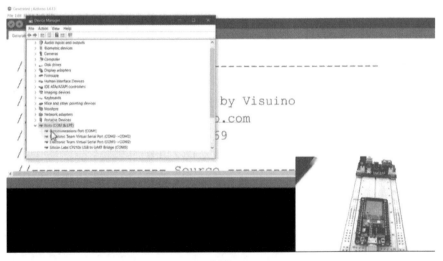

And from here, we go to ports and you can see that we have the silicon labs port connected to com five, now go here and select the board and go to E.S.P 32 Arduino.

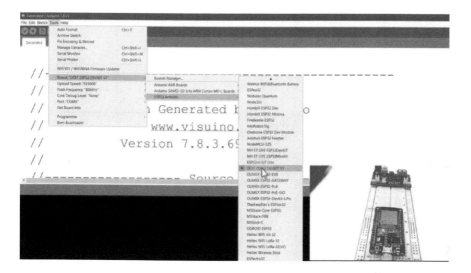

And from here, scroll until you reach the IT E.S.P 32 got Virgin one then going into Tool's port and make sure that the right component is selected.

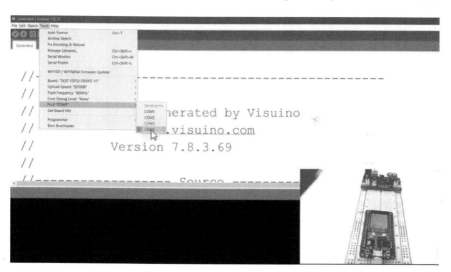

Com five now click upload. And I will press the mute button to make sure that the upload process.

```
//-----------------------------------------
//
//            Sketch Generated by Visuino
//                  www.visuino.com
//         |       Version 7.8.3.69
//
//------------------------ Source ----------
```

Global variables use 15364 bytes (4%)
esptool.py v2.6
Serial port COM5
Connecting....

OK, now writing to the RAM, then uploading, as you can see now, the uploading process is done. We need to reset the board, so we need to click this button. As you can see, the blue light is now blinking just like what we programmed using the visual, you know, using this pulse generator.

ARDUINO IDE INSTALLATION

Let's see how we now install the audio IDC to write code for ESB 8 2 6 6 and use P 32.

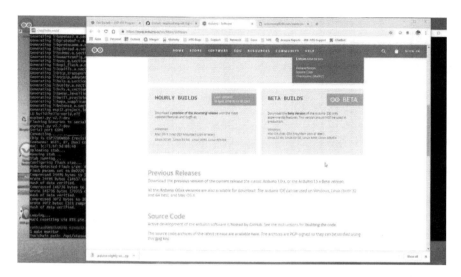

So what we need to do is to go to this website Ladino dot c c slash English main software. And when you come here we just click on the download button for the audio I.T. software that we need which in this case happens in my case because I'm using windows and when I click on the Windows software and download this I have just downloaded this already a few seconds back and it's in my directory here. There it is. So once you get this ordinary you begin to install this. So you right-click seven zip. I'm going to say extract here to audit on nightly windows and he's going to extract the whole Latino I.T. code here.

So I do know is an I.D. E allows us to write software and compile it and choose a board on which we would like to upload the software and finally upload it into the flash memory that of that board. Since we're talking about ESB 8 2 6 6 and the 32 will choose the right board and then write the code and upload the software. So that sort of makes it very useful for us to use Arduino I.D. So as you can see this has been already done almost and we're going to go into audit on nightly windows and we can then run this program. OK. Here we are. So our program will be Arduino dot EMC. I'll just give it a second more till it unzips completely. Yeah, there it is. So I go into this directory but I've unzipped this file and click on audio dot EMC. So this is a Windows standard laptop and I've installed no dot I.D. which is the latest nightly build from an ordinal Web site. So it does he goes it and brings it up here. Let's see. So once he brings it up we need to first load the Board Manager for the chipset we're using. So for that to do we have to go to preferences while preferences here and here you have to load

the Board Manager for ESB 8 2 6 6 which happens to be this I don't no dot ESB eight to six is dot com slash stables slash package ESB two systems dot com Jason File. So you click on this copy it and put it an additional board manages you are L and you say OK once you do this you can then go into tools and click on get click on board and boards manager he will then read this new Jason File and bring up all the boards that Jason File provides.

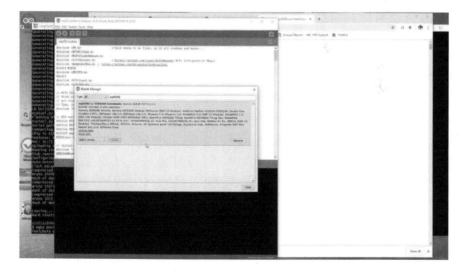

So he's reading it here and now we can look for ESB 8 to 6 6 and heavier since they're already installed it does not give an install button. But then in your case, you would just click on install here and it loads the ESB 8 2 6 6 board manager once having done that you have to go into tools and click the board which is your ESB 8 2 6 6 board

generic ESB 86 module or generic it 2 8 5 which you are a board that you have. And once you click on this you can then load any example that you want. So you can for that you go into a file you just loading that board and then you can go into file examples and you can just pick any basic example like blink rate and close the previous window and if you notice here that for that board he just has a blinking button you just bring the LCD and you can click on this checkbox here to compile the code or you can click on this button to upload the code to your board. So that's pretty simple. This is how Adorno can recognize your board. You can write code and upload it to it. We go into more details later on as we do the compiling upload just want to show you how to quickly install the audio idea.

ESP-IDF INSTALLATION

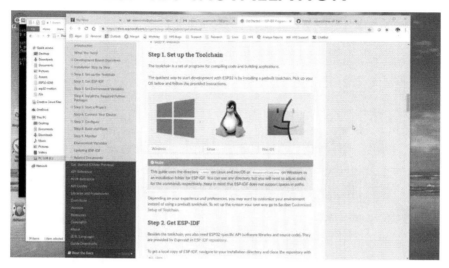

In the last project series, we have seen how to set up the idea for Arduino, and in this one, we're going to set up the ESB idea that allows developers to sit on top of the ESB idea directly without going through another Shim layer of Audio Api ice. And it sort of gives you more power so that you can use the ESB idea of API. So for that, we go into this dog to space of dot com slash project ESB IDF and we got to follow these two steps. The first step is that of the two which in itself. So since I'm on windows I'm going to open the windows page here and this sets up the toolchain. So for us to get these windows to we change and the meiosis to zip file you download the zip file here. And once you download the zip file you will get a terminal window which you can click on is

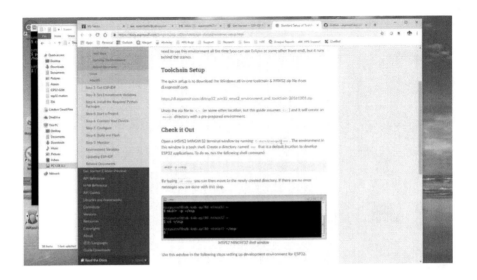

called mini Gateway 32 or EMC and you make a directory called ESB in that. So let's do these steps and then we can go back to step two. So once you download this file I just did it a few seconds back. You get this ESB three to win three to meiosis environment and the toolchain and you right-click on this and you say seven zip and you extract it here. So what this does is it makes you a directory called my size 32 and under this, it gives you all these files.

So here you have this supposed to open this term has been called many Gateway 32 dot EMC and once this opens up you are in this direction because your home directory slash from CTV is in my case this. The second step is to make a practical DSP that I just did. And what ESB once you do that the next step that is to be done is to clone the ESB IDF to which

is this one you to get clone recursive and get the whole ESB idea here and you say enter. So I don't do this and I'll read on this and it sort of gives you the complete practical the ESB IDF directly you put CBP the ESB IDF.

And this is a complete toolchain as well as the whole IDF. OK. So we got to step two done which is getting the lowliest IDF. Step three is environment variables 0 7 and I'm a biblical IDF bot to access this is ESB IDF directory and then you have to also the same directorate you have to install some biting variables which as you just say item minus M install equipment or. So if you want to see what this has. Let's look at what Python variables are there. You see more ideas or comments that you'll find.

These are the Python libraries that the dev environment wants for it to function properly which is Python serial future cryptography and then so once this source has to be installed by the by giving this command okay now facilities available I forgot to mention that you will open the windows the site here and go-go to this directory called my site 32 EDT provides the D create a new file they're called export IDF and enter this one line there. So that's how you set up the park and you're pretty much done right and you set up the ideal environment.

WIFI SNIFFER - 1

So we go back to a directory called ESB and under ESB we have various component examples. For example, let's look at this we made a hellhole earlier and now we've made a Wi-Fi e.g. example.

We go to Wi-Fi and you'll see that it has the same structure which is it has a built rectory ultimately when you combine it. It has one main directly which is mandatory to have a component under that you can make file and then these could confess are generated after you do a make. And if you go inside main you'll find your component or make fiber just generally empty and your Wi-Fi e.g. main door to see which is your main file of the application. So that is the structure of your lifeline program. OK. So let's stop looking at this program.

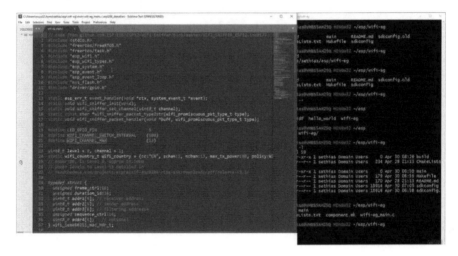

This is a very simple program. It just puts you through to a device like a chipset in a guessing mode and starts capturing packets. So as always we include free autos libraries autos what edge free autos tossed on the edge and so on. And also this time some Wi-Fi API.

We want to use a different vehicle to include some by Title X Files of so let's look at the main program first the app man that gets called as I mentioned earlier in the earlier project. The app man is the main task that gets called from the protocol CPO of the done with these toxic Busey to start. You want one of them we call the app main program running on the protocol. See you. So this is the main app's main task is running. We've been to fellow world and this is the main function my face different in it. Then I printed information that is the same as the last example. So can be sort of safely ignored all the wheel here. So the main thing here only was calling by sniffer in it. And we'll see what happens there and they'll be going to loop then start and go to start what we do is we wait for 500 milliseconds and we set the channel to which our number one. Initially, the channel is defined as one and we dwell on the channel for 500 milliseconds and we start getting callbacks and packets on that channel. Then off the final milliseconds, this delay completes and we switch the channel by plus one. So basically we are connected to two point four gigahertz. So plus one means it so there are 13 channels in 2.5 gigahertz but on the water lapping channels are only 1 6 and 11. So in my house, I have eight-point eleven G and N. So we only have three nonoverlapping channels. So if I said it to one and then I give this channel a channel this plus one it really skips to six and the next level then goes back to one. So we are sniffing back guess in Channel 1 6 and eleven and refined in milliseconds. So that's your main program. So the real meat of this program is in Wi-Fi sniffer.

f

Let's go back to the Wi-Fi sniffer in it and see what happens there. So first we do VMS flash and it just goes and initializes is the flash chip. Then we have to nationalize the TPP adapter in it. So we call this function which goes and implement. So what does it? It puts a ship layer above the current DCP stack which is right now LW IP but tomorrow you could go and change the stack from LW IP to something else. But because we're using the shim layer which is our DCP API is it doesn't matter what the unlink stack is you continue to something as tomorrow but because we're using an adapter then you have to keep our code the same then you have an ESB event loop in it. We're not using this here. If if you notice this looping it does what is used to get events from the chipset for example IP address and received our your Wi-Fi is connected or it's not connected. So all those events come and they get captured by the even handler which I have just put it as a simple function that turns the ESB OK but you could do magic here you can start getting events and they've done some things and act on it but we're not using that right now then this is the main function for Wi-Fi. We initialize the Wi-Fi we pass and if I fly in it config ECF g to pass the address of that and we call yes we might find in it you have to call this function before you can use any of the Wi-Fi API is then basic stuff set the countries at the storage we want to see if the variables set the Wi-Fi mode to null knowledge only use if you want to set the chipset into a promiscuous mode if you want to set it to station

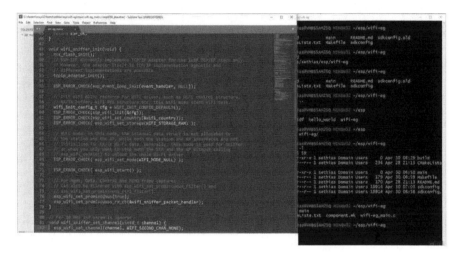

more AP More than you would use different to find here and finally you call ESB Wi-Fi stopped and just offer that you put the chip in promiscuous mode which allows you to receive data controlled my frames you don't get enter packets but you get all the other kinds of frames you can also whether we offer this call set a filter where you can only receive some sort some type of packet we're not done that we have to get every packet here and what you also tell the Wi-Fi chip is to whether we're packets are coming you call back dysfunctional Wi-Fi sniffer packet handler which I've written here is the sort of the main function that gets all the packets and doesn't print right and that function is here.

So this function is the function they're going to get all the packets and the packet type will be of which traveler type costs that do promise gets the packet. And we start building on stuff. Let me take a break here and come back with more details on this program.

WIFI SNIFFER - 2

We're looking at this Wi-Fi program which puts your chip into a promise guess more than you start getting callbacks into dysfunction by five different packet type sorry life sniffer packet handler with the package that the chip is receiving and sending to our application. So if you notice here we are getting a voice to our buff and also a packet type the packet type. If it's not management we just return we just taking management packets here and what you could do is anything you can do to get a packet and make it proper in a full-blown sniffer. This for example and should you. We are just interested in green packets and what I do is I take this buffer and I type promiscuous packet.

And the reason I do it is that if you look at this website Dr. Dot Com and you can look for any API search here which is relevant for ESB 32. This is what B structure that is returned to you. And it has two members it has a payload and hasn't had a Wi-Fi packet on its control it gives a lot more information about the packet being received like RSA society and channel number and so on for the patent bill of the project we take it off and it has the end of the Wi-Fi. I get the MAC addresses and so on and this gives us additional metadata. Let's just go into this guy. See this gives you our society.

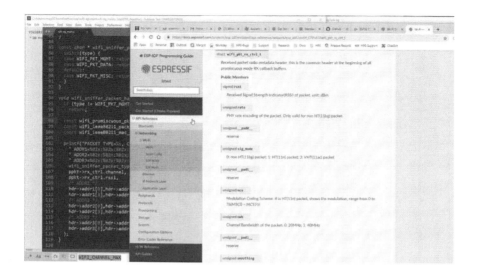

Read the packet of the seed padding information and stuff like that. So this is this doc is very important for us to use the API is very well to come back here. We can avoid our buffer be tied to this same buffer we just saw here. And from this buffer, we get the payload which we deposit to our packet which has defined the structure here itself. And from this same packet, we also get the header which is our header off the packet that's come from my five minutes all the inside information and stuff we can directly get from his buffer. The feedback that we can directly sort of point that to the actual artist control or channel I says we can bring those out like we're doing here. And for mac addresses, we dig the payload and we type it to our package structure here. And from this parking structure, we point to the header and we get the header.

Let's quickly go up and I'll tell you what I'm talking about here the editors. So the payload is this right. I'm sorry the payload is this one here which has the header and the payload and the header is what this is. So we can print on the MAC address and that stuff. This is here. So this is our main packet here. And this points to a header which is where there are all the other MAC addresses so this is standard able to live in a format that can be seen in any order to inspect. So I think complex here. So we just go in and go into header from header we come here and type on the MAC addresses we come back

here to the function if you notice here is what we did we got a white stripe buffer which was promised gives back at them which is B packet and from there we go to the payload we type to our IT rural of impact and we again sort of get the pointer and get the header. Right now we start building on stuff the MAC addresses the RSA society. And just take a printout of what we're receiving. So that's pretty much it. It's a very simple you know three function program and you can be converted your E B 32 into a Wi-Fi sniffer and you could look at all sorts of data coming in and act on it and write wonderful applications using it. So in the next week, you will run this application and we'll see how this goes.

WIFI SNIFFER - 3

So we're in this Wi-Fi example. We do a make flash and we make monitor and this is what we get and they make money. Just in the controls of this window so it doesn't go that fast.

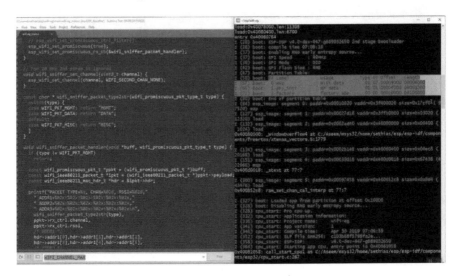

You know it gives you a standard output as the data put up it gives your platform partition table and then it loads the image here and then here you have the blue-chip you that are starting up here. And then finally off the Wi-Fi driver task that's getting initialized here. When you do Wi-Fi in it it is also initialized as the X and RDX buffers and stuff like that.

It gives me 32 and it goes into a sniffer. And remember here we done that you print out hello world that you would you print. You know that is the core is between two chips and then we start doing the lighting or the management frames here. So look at this is Piper's management.

It's only collecting type management frames it's giving the channel information for 500 milliseconds. We notice it remains Channel 1 and then jumps to Channel Eleven thirty-six. And then Channel Eleven. So I didn't keep it long enough I guess but this is what happens it's just jumping from Channel 1 6 and 11 and it starts getting all the packets that are management frames going to destination addresses the source addresses this and you can print out all the information like our society is and go right again.

So we get an idea of what's going on here to make a monitor which connects to the USB cable and the chipset and starts collecting all the information being sent on the USP. So while he's doing that we can quickly go back here and see this is what I was printing here and bringing the packet type channel and you can pick up all kinds of information that you find interesting from here.

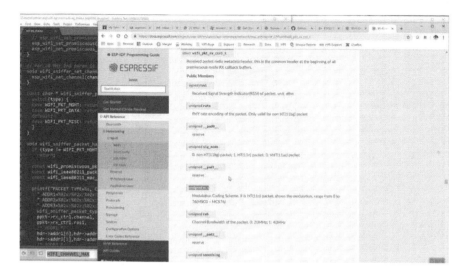

Like the rate at which is being sent the modulation scheme and stuff like that there's just too much stuff that you can do a print out normally management but all kinds of data frames and you can pin them all in this function here along with all the addresses and this is what it has become done here. This is where I was spending other stuff. So this is just starting. And if you notice here is that on channel number one for final seconds and it jumps is supposed to sort of maybe it's only Channel 1 being broadcast here.

So it's not getting packets and others I guess.

And we do see so this is pretty much it.

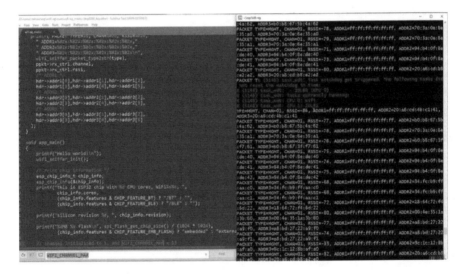

Guys I know I would encourage you to play around with this and see what happens and you see a voice not getting triggered you have to give it time to go in back to the watchdog I guess and that's why this is happening so we will look at this later than the other projects of why this is happening. So everything is working on the Wi-Fi is running on CBS 0 and this one is idle and the watchdog time word came up on the idea of a CPO zeal for some reason it's got triggered so it will be hard to see why it didn't get time to bet the watchdog on what we can do about it. Otherwise great. I hope you enjoyed this.

EXAMPLE CODE

// code from github.com/ESP-EOS/ESP32-WiFi-Sniffer/blob/master/WIFI_SNIFFER_ESP32.ino#L77

```c
#include <stdio.h>

#include "freertos/FreeRTOS.h"

#include "freertos/task.h"

#include "esp_wifi.h"

#include "esp_wifi_types.h"

#include "esp_system.h"

#include "esp_event.h"

#include "esp_event_loop.h"

#include "nvs_flash.h"

#include "driver/gpio.h"

static esp_err_t event_handler(void *ctx, system_event_t *event);

static void wifi_sniffer_init(void);

static void wifi_sniffer_set_channel(uint8_t channel);

static const char *wifi_sniffer_packet_type2str(wifi_promiscuous_pkt_type_t type);

static void wifi_sniffer_packet_handler(void *buff, wifi_promiscuous_pkt_type_t type);
```

```c
#define LED_GPIO_PIN        5

#define WIFI_CHANNEL_SWITCH_INTERVAL  (500)

#define WIFI_CHANNEL_MAX    (13)

uint8_t level = 0, channel = 1;

static wifi_country_t wifi_country = {cc:"CN", schan:1, nchan:13, max_tx_power:80, policy:WIFI_COUNTRY_POLICY_AUTO};

// power:80, is Level 0, approx 19.5dBm
// power levels to Level is detailed in
// readthedocs.com/projects/espressif-esp8266-rtos-sdk/downloads/pdf/release-v3.1/

typedef struct {
 unsigned frame_ctrl:16;
 unsigned duration_id:16;
 uint8_t addr1[6]; // receiver address
 uint8_t addr2[6]; // sender address
 uint8_t addr3[6]; // filtering address+
 unsigned sequence_ctrl:16;
 uint8_t addr4[6];  // optional
} wifi_ieee80211_mac_hdr_t;

typedef struct {
 wifi_ieee80211_mac_hdr_t hdr;
 uint8_t payload[0]; // network data + checksum
```

```c
} wifi_ieee80211_packet_t;

esp_err_t event_handler(void *ctx, system_event_t *event) {
    return ESP_OK;
}

void wifi_sniffer_init(void) {
    nvs_flash_init();
    // ESP-IDF currently implements TCP/IP Adapter for the lwIP TCP/IP stack only.
    // However, the adapter itself is TCP/IP implementation agnostic and
    // different implementations are possible.
    tcpip_adapter_init();
    ESP_ERROR_CHECK(esp_event_loop_init(event_handler, NULL));
    // Init WiFi Alloc resource for WiFi driver, such as WiFi control structure,
    // RX/TX buffer, WiFi NVS structure etc, this WiFi also start WiFi task.
    wifi_init_config_t cfg = WIFI_INIT_CONFIG_DEFAULT();
    ESP_ERROR_CHECK(esp_wifi_init(&cfg));
    ESP_ERROR_CHECK(esp_wifi_set_country(&wifi_country));
    ESP_ERROR_CHECK( esp_wifi_set_storage(WIFI_STORAGE_RAM) );
    // NULL mode: in this mode, the internal data struct is not allocated to
    // the station and the AP, while both the station and AP interfaces are not
    // initialized for RX/TX Wi-Fi data. Generally, this mode is used for Sniffer,
```

```c
    // or when you only want to stop both the STA and the AP without calling
    // esp_wifi_deinit() to unload the whole Wi-Fi driver.
    ESP_ERROR_CHECK( esp_wifi_set_mode(WIFI_MODE_NULL) );
    ESP_ERROR_CHECK( esp_wifi_start() );
    // For Mgmt, Data, Control and MIMO frame captures
    // Can also be filtered with esp_wifi_set_promiscuous_filter() and
    // esp_wifi_set_promiscuous_ctrl_filter().
    esp_wifi_set_promiscuous(true);
    esp_wifi_set_promiscuous_rx_cb(&wifi_sniffer_packet_handler);
}

// For 20 MHz 2nd param is ignored
void wifi_sniffer_set_channel(uint8_t channel) {
    esp_wifi_set_channel(channel, WIFI_SECOND_CHAN_NONE);
}

const char * wifi_sniffer_packet_type2str(wifi_promiscuous_pkt_type_t type) {
    switch(type) {
    case WIFI_PKT_MGMT: return "MGMT";
    case WIFI_PKT_DATA: return "DATA";
    default:
    case WIFI_PKT_MISC: return "MISC";
    }
}
```

```
}
void wifi_sniffer_packet_handler(void *buff,
wifi_promiscuous_pkt_type_t type) {

if (type != WIFI_PKT_MGMT)

  return;

const wifi_promiscuous_pkt_t *ppkt = (wifi_promiscuous_pkt_t *)buff;

const wifi_ieee80211_packet_t *ipkt = (wifi_ieee80211_packet_t *)ppkt->payload;

const wifi_ieee80211_mac_hdr_t *hdr = &ipkt->hdr;

printf("PACKET TYPE=%s, CHAN=%02d, RSSI=%02d,"

" ADDR1=%02x:%02x:%02x:%02x:%02x:%02x,"

" ADDR2=%02x:%02x:%02x:%02x:%02x:%02x,"

" ADDR3=%02x:%02x:%02x:%02x:%02x:%02x\n",

wifi_sniffer_packet_type2str(type),

ppkt->rx_ctrl.channel,

ppkt->rx_ctrl.rssi,

/* ADDR1 */

hdr->addr1[0],hdr->addr1[1],hdr->addr1[2],

hdr->addr1[3],hdr->addr1[4],hdr->addr1[5],

/* ADDR2 */

hdr->addr2[0],hdr->addr2[1],hdr->addr2[2],

hdr->addr2[3],hdr->addr2[4],hdr->addr2[5],
```

```c
    /* ADDR3 */
    hdr->addr3[0],hdr->addr3[1],hdr->addr3[2],
    hdr->addr3[3],hdr->addr3[4],hdr->addr3[5]
    );
}
void app_main()
{
    printf("Hello world!\n");
    wifi_sniffer_init();
    /* Print chip information */
    esp_chip_info_t chip_info;
    esp_chip_info(&chip_info);
    printf("This is ESP32 chip with %d CPU cores, WiFi%s%s, ",
        chip_info.cores,
        (chip_info.features & CHIP_FEATURE_BT) ? "/BT" : "",
        (chip_info.features & CHIP_FEATURE_BLE) ? "/BLE" : "");
    printf("silicon revision %d, ", chip_info.revision);
    printf("%dMB %s flash\n", spi_flash_get_chip_size() / (1024 * 1024),
        (chip_info.features & CHIP_FEATURE_EMB_FLASH) ? "embedded" : "external");
    // channel initialized to 1, and WIFI_CHANNEL_MAX = 13
```

```
// 2.4 GHz (802.11b/g/n/ax) - has 14 channels in 2.4 GHz, with 22 Mhz spacing

// we get with 802.11 g,n - 1,6,11 mom overlapping channels

for (int i = 0; i<=20; i++) {

vTaskDelay(WIFI_CHANNEL_SWITCH_INTERVAL / portTICK_PERIOD_MS);

wifi_sniffer_set_channel(channel);

channel = (channel % WIFI_CHANNEL_MAX) + 1;

}
}
```

OLED ESP32 DISPLAY PART1

So in this third sample project are going to be trying to interface this whole ID display module with our ESB 32. So again we are working with our last example which was by a fine example written and we will extend that with this component driver that can support this all LED display as the 1 3 0 6 modules. OK.

So what I did was I went into Google in a social down and I found that this is one driver is B 32 squared C assistive 1 3 0 6. That's the driver for ESB IDF that can support this module. And since I didn't want the C++ library I clicked on this branch and I got the B or C download and I downloaded these files into the way to include this component in I work it gets in our Wi-Fi directory is we just want the main directory if you click on Main and you download these files and these are the

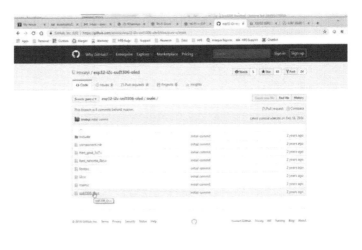

ones that you put under a component directory in our Wi-Fi module. So if you look at directory structure right now we had made a directory called by file so I mean a new one called by Wi-Fi led and under that you have built components make file mean etc. This is what was existing and components were sort of empty right down to under the compressed directory. I did a clone of this directory to remove all the unnecessary files and ultimately what you will have under components is the 1 3 0 6 parent. And underneath this, I have all the files that I mean directly will include file that has to be included by our file which is existing under me which is a by file so I include I have fonts on the edges quite see Dot agents as 2 1 3 0 6 dotage which is nothing but under this you have the interactivity has the three files. So basically just put everything under the mean inside. It says 1 3 0 6 under components and we are good to go. OK so let's go here and you would have done under my fake wallet.

I already had the main direction and the components were empty. So two components but I have assessed 2 1 3 0 6 and a number 7 in all the files that I just showed you. That's the drapery structure.

ESP32 DISPLAY PART2

This is the next part of integrating the SSD 1 3 2 1 3 0 6 that led the speed of the ECB 3 2 and this is the smart piece of code that you've written so you've taken the earlier by for example and in that

included the SS 1 3 0 6 h file that is here and that's pretty much it. And it does include. And you go down to our main admin function and include this quote which was I copied from GitHub. If you look at GitHub there's already the main door to see that that point is an example of how to use this.

And from this admin, I copied that. This goes in Prince Andrew we have 32 Adventure Box and uses this API is that provided by this driver. So pretty simple just include this. These lines of code that draw rectangles like the font use API as an end. This is angular does and let it function that I'm calling from my app mean. Here it is and we're done. This is how we integrate now in terms of what had done in terms of integrating it physically. I put the FDA and a Klines it says it is a two-pin depends on the wallet. I put them on GPA opens 22 and 21. It has 1 BTC and background thing so it's got 4 pins. It's very simple to integrate and that sets that speed up.

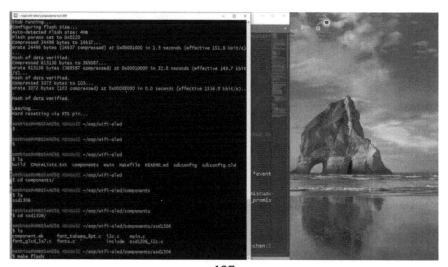

Before that, all you could do to make this work is to make flash and then automatically compiles your main file as well as the components and as prepares the whole sketch for 4 uploads to be 32. Great.

OLED ESP32 DISPLAY PART3

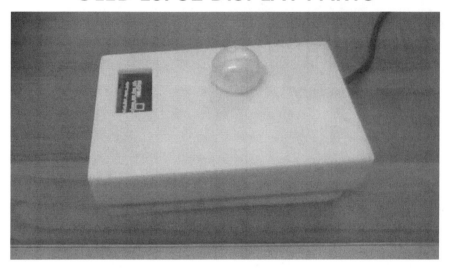

So now you can see the eyes quite see this place looking fine as quoted in the last example.

EXAMPLE CODE

```
// code from github.com/ESP-EOS/ESP32-WiFi-Sniffer/blob/master/WIFI_SNIFFER_ESP32.ino#L77

#include <stdio.h>

#include "freertos/FreeRTOS.h"

#include "freertos/task.h"

#include "esp_wifi.h"

#include "esp_wifi_types.h"

#include "esp_system.h"

#include "esp_event.h"

#include "esp_event_loop.h"

#include "nvs_flash.h"

#include "driver/gpio.h"

#include "esp_log.h" // for ESP_LOGE

// Initialize the OLED display using Wire library

// cd wifi-oled/components/

// git clone --single-branch --branch pure-c https://github.com/imxieyi/esp32-i2c-ssd1306-oled.git

// Delete all files in this report except for "main"

// Then move all files under "main" up one level

#include "ssd1306.h"

//SSD1306Wire display(0x3c, 21, 22); // SDA, SCK
```

```c
static esp_err_t event_handler(void *ctx, system_event_t *event);

static void wifi_sniffer_init(void);

static void wifi_sniffer_set_channel(uint8_t channel);

static const char *wifi_sniffer_packet_type2str(wifi_promiscuous_pkt_type_t type);

static void wifi_sniffer_packet_handler(void *buff, wifi_promiscuous_pkt_type_t type);

#define LED_GPIO_PIN     5

#define WIFI_CHANNEL_SWITCH_INTERVAL  (500)

#define WIFI_CHANNEL_MAX     (13)

uint8_t level = 0, channel = 1;

static wifi_country_t wifi_country = {cc:"CN", schan:1, nchan:13, max_tx_power:80, policy:WIFI_COUNTRY_POLICY_AUTO};

// power:80, is Level 0, approx 19.5dBm

// power levels to Level is detailed in

// readthedocs.com/projects/espressif-esp8266-rtos-sdk/downloads/pdf/release-v3.1/

typedef struct {

 unsigned frame_ctrl:16;

 unsigned duration_id:16;

 uint8_t addr1[6]; // receiver address

 uint8_t addr2[6]; // sender address

 uint8_t addr3[6]; // filtering address+
```

```c
  unsigned sequence_ctrl:16;

  uint8_t addr4[6]; // optional

} wifi_ieee80211_mac_hdr_t;

typedef struct {

  wifi_ieee80211_mac_hdr_t hdr;

  uint8_t payload[0]; // network data + checksum

} wifi_ieee80211_packet_t;

esp_err_t event_handler(void *ctx, system_event_t *event) {

  return ESP_OK;

}

void wifi_sniffer_init(void) {

  nvs_flash_init();

  // ESP-IDF currently implements TCP/IP Adapter for the lwIP TCP/IP stack only.
  // However, the adapter itself is TCP/IP implementation agnostic and
  // different implementations are possible.

  tcpip_adapter_init();

  ESP_ERROR_CHECK(esp_event_loop_init(event_handler, NULL));

  // Init WiFi Alloc resource for WiFi driver, such as WiFi control structure,
  // RX/TX buffer, WiFi NVS structure etc, this WiFi also start WiFi task.

  wifi_init_config_t cfg = WIFI_INIT_CONFIG_DEFAULT();

  ESP_ERROR_CHECK(esp_wifi_init(&cfg));
```

```
ESP_ERROR_CHECK(esp_wifi_set_country(&wifi_country));
ESP_ERROR_CHECK( esp_wifi_set_storage(WIFI_STORAGE_RAM) );


// NULL mode: in this mode, the internal data struct is not allocated to
// the station and the AP, while both the station and AP interfaces are not
// initialized for RX/TX Wi-Fi data. Generally, this mode is used for Sniffer,
// or when you only want to stop both the STA and the AP without calling
// esp_wifi_deinit() to unload the whole Wi-Fi driver.
ESP_ERROR_CHECK( esp_wifi_set_mode(WIFI_MODE_NULL) );
ESP_ERROR_CHECK( esp_wifi_start() );
// For Mgmt, Data, Control and MIMO frame captures
// Can also be filtered with esp_wifi_set_promiscuous_filter() and
// esp_wifi_set_promiscuous_ctrl_filter().
esp_wifi_set_promiscuous(true);
esp_wifi_set_promiscuous_rx_cb(&wifi_sniffer_packet_handler);
}
// For 20 MHz 2nd param is ignored
void wifi_sniffer_set_channel(uint8_t channel) {
    esp_wifi_set_channel(channel, WIFI_SECOND_CHAN_NONE);
}
```

```c
const char * wifi_sniffer_packet_type2str(wifi_promiscuous_pkt_type_t type) {

switch(type) {

case WIFI_PKT_MGMT: return "MGMT";

case WIFI_PKT_DATA: return "DATA";

default:

case WIFI_PKT_MISC: return "MISC";

}

}

void wifi_sniffer_packet_handler(void *buff, wifi_promiscuous_pkt_type_t type) {

if (type != WIFI_PKT_MGMT)

  return;

const wifi_promiscuous_pkt_t *ppkt = (wifi_promiscuous_pkt_t *)buff;

const wifi_ieee80211_packet_t *ipkt = (wifi_ieee80211_packet_t *)ppkt->payload;

const wifi_ieee80211_mac_hdr_t *hdr = &ipkt->hdr;

printf("PACKET TYPE=%s, CHAN=%02d, RSSI=%02d,"

" ADDR1=%02x:%02x:%02x:%02x:%02x:%02x,"

" ADDR2=%02x:%02x:%02x:%02x:%02x:%02x,"

" ADDR3=%02x:%02x:%02x:%02x:%02x:%02x\n",

wifi_sniffer_packet_type2str(type),
```

```
            ppkt->rx_ctrl.channel,
            ppkt->rx_ctrl.rssi,
            /* ADDR1 */

            hdr->addr1[0],hdr->addr1[1],hdr->addr1[2],
            hdr->addr1[3],hdr->addr1[4],hdr->addr1[5],
            /* ADDR2 */
            hdr->addr2[0],hdr->addr2[1],hdr->addr2[2],
            hdr->addr2[3],hdr->addr2[4],hdr->addr2[5],
            /* ADDR3 */
            hdr->addr3[0],hdr->addr3[1],hdr->addr3[2],
            hdr->addr3[3],hdr->addr3[4],hdr->addr3[5]
        );
}
void oled_init() {
    if (ssd1306_init(0, 22, 21)) { //SDA, SCK
        ESP_LOGI("OLED", "oled inited");
        ssd1306_draw_rectangle(0, 10, 30, 20, 20, 1);
        ssd1306_select_font(0, 0);
        ssd1306_draw_string(0, 0, 0, "glcd_5x7_font_info", 1, 0);
        ssd1306_select_font(0, 1);
        ssd1306_draw_string(0, 0, 18, "tahoma_8pt_font_info", 1, 0);
```

```
        ssd1306_draw_string(0, 55, 30, "Hello ESP32!", 1, 0);
        ssd1306_refresh(0, true);
    } else {
        ESP_LOGE("OLED", "oled init failed");


    }
}
void app_main()
{
    printf("Hello world!\n");
    wifi_sniffer_init();
    oled_init();
    /* Print chip information */
    esp_chip_info_t chip_info;
    esp_chip_info(&chip_info);
    printf("This is ESP32 chip with %d CPU cores, WiFi%s%s, ",
        chip_info.cores,
        (chip_info.features & CHIP_FEATURE_BT) ? "/BT" : "",
        (chip_info.features & CHIP_FEATURE_BLE) ? "/BLE" : "");
    printf("silicon revision %d, ", chip_info.revision);
    printf("%dMB %s flash\n", spi_flash_get_chip_size() / (1024 * 1024),
```

```
            (chip_info.features & CHIP_FEATURE_EMB_FLASH) ? "embedded" : "external");

   // channel initialized to 1, and WIFI_CHANNEL_MAX = 13

   // 2.4 GHz (802.11b/g/n/ax) - has 14 channels in 2.4 GHz, with 22 Mhz spacing

   // we get with 802.11 g,n - 1,6,11 mom overlapping channels


   for (int i = 0; i<=20; i++) {
   vTaskDelay(WIFI_CHANNEL_SWITCH_INTERVAL / portTICK_PERIOD_MS);
   wifi_sniffer_set_channel(channel);
   channel = (channel % WIFI_CHANNEL_MAX) + 1;
   }
}
```

CREATE A NEW EMAIL ACCOUNT TO BE USED AS SENDER

I'm going to explain to you how you can create a send that e-mail. First, you need to go to [REMOVED] dot com. And since I already have an account, I have to create the account. Now, who will most likely be directed to a page like this? Click on Create Account for me. Now, let's right all information to start creating our GAO slightly educational engineering a do you NJ team and write your passwords. Then conferment and click next. Once you click next, you'll be asked to enter your mobile number and your recovery email address. I will enter my recovery email address without my phone number and you need to enter your birth information. Then television, the. Now click next. Once you click next, you can click, I agree to their terms of service. That's it. This is our new e-mail account. And you need to make sure that you have. Your e-mail name is incorrect. Now there is one more step that you need to do before moving forward. You need to open up or allow less secure access to your [REMOVED] account. This is a timber account. You shouldn't use it for, let's say, personal e-mailing because you'll allow less secure access so that, yes, people can access this account and send e-mails using this account. To do that, you need to go. And right, G.M. lists secured ups and Google or anywhere. Now, as you can see, you'll give this my account at Google. Com slash list. Secure apps click once. And make sure that you are using the right email account, which is this one. As you can see, u you n GTM English Jamila's, come and click this sign. Now, once you click this sign, as you can see, and this description, some apps, and devices use this secure sign-in technology, which makes your account vulnerable. You can turn off access for these apps which Google recommends, or turn it on if you want to use them, despite the risks. And we want to use them despite the risks.

Goodwill automatically turns into this setting off if it is not being used. That's why it was off. Now, we did turn it on because we want to allow the E.S.P board to access our email account easily without issues, because, you know, when you access your [REMOVED] account from unknown devices, you get the Google treats it as a security threat. So we are allowing Lisick your apps to get access to this news e-mail account so that we can send emails. Now. In the next lesson, we are going to start coding and I'll add more information about US and TB server settings for email outlook and Hotmail accounts. But that's it for this lesson on what you need to do is create an account, a new account and allow lists, secure app access.

SMTP SERVER SETTINGS

S empty P server settings. Now, as I already mentioned, each of these TB server providers provides settings for you to use. And in case you are using [REMOVED] account, these are thus MTBE server details that server domain is some TV, the G.M. dot com. Those are name is complete G.M. address. You have to write your e-mail address in full, like the Ashenoff Ijima loss column and the password. You have to write your e-mail password as well. Now, if you are using T.L. US ports, you have to use 587. And if you are using this as a port certificate, you have to use 465. And we are going to use SSL. So we're using 500 or four hundred sixty-five. Now is it required to use to us or is this all he has? It's required and it's enabled by default in the mail client library. That we already mentioned. Now, if you are using life or Hotmail as MTBE server settings, these are the server settings for live or Hotmail accounts, as MTV does like that come and you have to use your full address at lives at home or Hotmail that. Com. And here you have to write your password. This is the port number five hundred eighty-seven and it's required to have us. And as I said, certificates for your mailing client. Now for Outlook users or Outlook accounts, you have to write some TBD at Office 365. Dotcom. Write your full email at Outlook dot com and your password, then yours 587 as a post and you are also required to use T.L. US and assets are enabled, mail client. Now, in case your mail server wasn't one of these, you need to search for some TB server settings. Now you have everything you need to start sending emails using E.S.P bonds. So in the next lessons, the fuel coming lessons, we are going to learn how to code your E.S.P board to start sending e-mails.

CODING THE ESP32 EMAIL ALERT PROJECT

NTPC server with SDM or text or any other thing that you want to send. Now, for the sake of testing, we are only sending an email once when they SPF 30 to bald boots and we can change this later depending on our project or our specific properties or what we want. Now you should be able to create the code easily. I will go with you in a step-by-step manner and we will start by creating a new Arduino project. Then let's save this project. To make sure that we save our work. Let's call it to the cord.

Now, the first thing that we need to do is include some libraries. So we'll start with hashtag include, then we can add the library name, which is E.S.P. Thirsted to underscore main client, the texts, which is the library that we did use the managed libraries. We did that in a previous lesson. They make a lands library. Now we need to insert our network credentials. So let's add two variables. The first one is a constant character for the network credential as I.D. and my network name as a show on TV. And we also need to enter a password. So we'll have to write constant characters. Passwords. And we'd have to enter our password. And on three islands, but my personal, but I will. Okay, I will use this one now we need to enter our e-mail settings. Sorry to enter that email and that account and the password for the e-mails and that account. So you need to define your variables. So the slide defines e-mail sender count. And we already know that our e-mail is the U. N. Angie team had G.M. dot com. Now we also have to define the password. So e-mail sender. Passwords. We need to enter the password tier.

```
#include "ESP32_MailClient.h"

const char* ssid = "Ashraf TV ";
const char* password = "asm@05666600099";

#define emailSenserAccount "eduengteamen@gmail.com"
#define emailSenderPassword "Password"
```

I want to write it. I would like to point off this thing. Now you want to enter or you must enter that a C e-mail account or the one who will that e-mail account from your E.S.P board. This is the e-mail that will receive the e-mail sent by our ISP to do that by define and invite email sibilant. Then write the e-mail. I will send the emails to mine. Do you team G.M. come, which is ARSH? Shall e-mail. OK. Now you need to enter your this and TB settings. And we did explain in the previous lesson that it's empty B server settings for G mail outlook and Hotmail account. There are constant values provided by each of these companies. So you just need to copy unbiased values. And since we are using g mail, it will be easy. Now let's start by adding some TB servers. So I define then as an MTBE server and assumed it to be the G.M. that's come next, we need to assign the board for this some TV server. So I define a simple TV server first and then write the number four hundred sixty-five. Now we need to write the email subject so we can also use define, define e-mail subject. And we can but E.S.P. Certa to this thing.

```
#define emailSenserAccount "eduengteamen@gmail.com"
#define emailSenderPassword "Password"
#define emailRecipient "eduengteam@gmail.com"
#define smtpServer "smtp.gmail.com"
#define smptServerPort 465
#define emailSubject "ESP32 Testing Email"

void setup() {
```

E-mail now that we have done all of this. We need to create an awesome TB data object and we can call it TB data that contains the data to send via email and all other configurations. So simply light some TB data and name it as TB data. That's it. Now, inside, you've set up. This is for the configuration before the up function. Now, inside the setup, we need to start the Wi-Fi connection using lifeguarded begin and we need to pass the ASUS idea for the network and the password to make sure that it will connect to our local Wi-Fi network. Now. We will use an if. Why not? If statement aside, to make sure that we give yes people time to connect so onside. This we are going to use the state of Misho status if it's not equal. Are connected, then it means that Wi-Fi is not connected yet. And in that case, for debugging, we can print something. We can print a dot or a start. Then you need to add some delay to give it enough time to connect.

```
SMTPData smtpData;

void setup() {
  // put your setup code here, to run once:
WiFi.begin(ssid, password);
while(WiFi.status() != WL_CONNECTED)
{
    Serial.print();
  }
```

Now, if it's not connected, it will keep printing stars until it connects. Maybe your Wi-Fi is offline. All you have is a name. Is this idea or password are wrong. Now. After that. After we finish checking and making sure that we are connecting to our Wi-Fi network inside the setup, we need to set Arlis MTV data to object details. So you must cite some T.B. data. Dot Sick Logan. We need to see that again, information that we already defined here. So we will start with the first one or chaise an MTBE server. In that case, it's a Google server and we need that server bought 70 be server bought and we need the e-mails and that account. And leave that e-mail sender password. So we need to pass all of these four values to this MTBE that I object to after that we need to sit that, send our name, and send that email. So. We can't use this MTV data. That sits in the function and will take E.S.P filled at all, whatever want to name it. Then we can provide that email sendup account.

```
{
    Serial.print("*");
    delay(200);
}
smtpData.setLogin(smtpServer, smtpServerPort, emailSenderAccoun
smtpData.setSender("ESP32 Sender", emailSenderAccount);
}

void loop() {
```

Now we need to send the e-mail priority and we have a tie, low or medium. It's something you can't ignore. But I prefer adding high priority to make sure that it will send it as a high priority e-mail. Now you can enter high, low, medium, or you can use numbers. OK. After doing that, we canceled the email subject. So polite as MTBE data that sits subject the subject for our email and we will use the one that we ordered defined. E-mail subject. We'll define this here. E-mail subject. So we are using these variables. Now. We need to send the message itself. So we need to use some TV data that it Mrs. And decide to cut right plaintext like Hallowell. This is, yes, an e-mail. This thing.

```
}
smtpData.setLogin(smtpServer, smtpServerPort, emailSenderAccoun
smtpData.setSender("ESP32 Sender", emailSenderAccount);
smtpData.setPriority("High");
smtpData.setSubject(emailSubject);
smtpData.setMessage("Hellow World This is ESP Email Testi");
}

void loop() {
```

To send the raw data and here to add false here, or you can send SDM al data and you are going to explain this in the next project. But that's it for this lesson. Let's summarize. We included that E.S.P main client library, the Wi-Fi network name, and the password that's in that account email. That's in the password that sealed the account. The one who received the message. The TB server information on port and the e-mail subject. After that, we started the Wi-Fi connection process and we waited until Wi-Fi is connected. We can add a line here. We can say serial. The print Wi-Fi is connected. Connected, then we passed the MTV server. Details. So this that object that we already defined here as some TV data we did said that information the sender e-mail the priority of this e-mail. The email subject. And the message in plain text. That's it. For all this, listen to your next and watch Cynic's less on what you are going to continue writing. Our very first called for e-mail alerts using the E.S.P board.

Now that we have created a plaintext e-mail, let's learn how to create it. A message in SDM. You will use the very same clothing data. That's the message. And inside here, you will add your text annual add through to means you will be are passing ASTM, and code false means you are passing plain text. Now, since we did right through here, through all the comments we can add. SDMI, Lecourtier and other Schimel code. We have to get as Jamal called to begin with. So we'll hear right. Estriol online code editor. And you can use this one or this one. W3 School. All of the online code editors. This one.

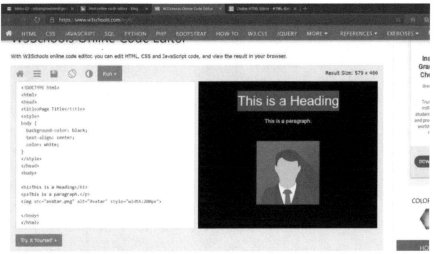

So if we want to use this one. As you can see, this is the online editor for this Web site. You can write your text and. Light here and see it here. See what's happening here.

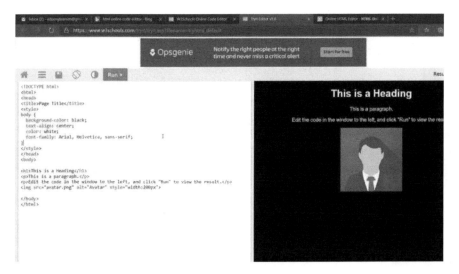

So all this takes to Canada, the heading, this is the headings. You could write your name and click run and will be visible here. Same for other things. Or you can simply try this one. You can start writing Hello, World.

E.S.P 30 to e-mail this thing, and you can simply Corbi this code. This is the human code for this line. You can add other information you plan.

A line that takes to be in the middle, you can increase the font size or change the font color. You can choose different formats if you want to make it as heading as you can see. It's more the background color. And it's colorful, the text itself. Now you can copy all of this and simply base it inside your code. Right. Click on Kobe, then go inside your code. Base it right here. As you can see, this is all a sham alcalde. Now. You can use this or you can use that or text. It's up to you. In my case, I will start with the raw text. Then we can test with ASTM. Now, let's move on with cord editing. Now, the final step is sitting the recipient email address. So right. Is empty. B, that that ad sibilant. And inside it. All right. Email me sibilant. That's it now that we have, all the details of this TB data. We are ready to send the email. So to send the email. You need to write if. Statement. And inside that, if you need to write this man, fly on that, send an email. We are using the send email function and we are passing this MTV data that we already filled here. And these lines. Now. After that, we can plant Syria, not plant on. There is an adult. We can't see it.

```
smtpData.setMessage("Hellow World This is ESP Email Testing",
//smtpData.setMessage("<h2 style="text-align: center;"><span s
//<h2 style="text-align: center;"><span style="background-colc
smtpData.addRecipient(emailRecipient);

if(!MailClient.sendMail(smtpData))
   Serial.println("Error in Sending the Email" + MailClient.smt
}
```

In sending the e-mail and we can give the code from the mail mainland, you can light mail client dot as MTBE erodes. Reason. This is how you can give that email it off. It will most likely print out a code that you can look up using Google to know exactly what's the problem. After sending the email, you can clear all the data from this empty, be that object. And we can do this using one symbol line, which is an awesome TB that is that empty. The empty function is the one that we can use to send empty emails. Now we are sending the email and the stuff function. This means that the email will be sent once and you have to pause to unplug, then blog it again. They ask people to send another email if they want to send the email more than once. You can simply use this method. Send email method inside the loop function. Now, for example, the loop function is empty. Now, we can start this thing, this court out, but we can add even more stuff in the law function now, you can create a callback function to give the email sending status to do that. That is a very. Easy method, you can simply define a callback function like the void. Let me show it to you. Let's create and your function and name it sends. Call back. Now. The synth callback function will have a simple chord. We are going to write the Syrian Mertle blend. And here we are going to write the message that in four. And we need to pass the message here.

```
  // put your main code here, to run repeatedly:

}


void sendCallback()
{
   Serial.println(msg.info());
  }
```

Send us a message now when the city's mother is sent. We covered the UNEF statement, and this statement will include the message his success in sending. Then we need to write. I think for the bugging inside, okay, we carve out plus signs.

```
}


void sendCallback(SendStatus message)
{
   Serial.println(message.info());

   if(message.success()){Serial.print("++++++++");}
  }
```

This means that the message was sent successfully. Otherwise, the message will we will get caught in all of us. A.B. Errol Reason poured on our cereal, Myrtle. Now, this is how you can create a callback function to give the email sending status. Sorry. Now, that's it. What you need to do next is very simple. You need to verify the code to make sure that it doesn't have any errors. Then we will upload the code to our E.S.P board. It will take a few seconds to come by the code.

```
smtpData.setLogin(smtpServer, smtpServerPort, emailSenderAccou
smtpData.setSender("ESP32 Sender", emailSenderAccount);
smtpData.setPriority("High");
smtpData.setSubject(emailSubject);
smtpData.setMessage("Hellow World This is ESP Email Testing",
//smtpData.setMessage("<h2 style="text-align: center;"><span s
//<h2 style="text-align: center;"><span style="background-colo
smtpData.addRecipient(emailRecipient);
```

```
exit status 1
'smtpServerPort' was not declared in this scope
```

Okay, as you can see here, have an arrow, as A.B. said, of port was not defined in this school. Let's make sure that we have. Right. As A.P. several posts. Oh, we have to spill some T.P. Let's go back and fix it. As MTV said, what post? Okay. That's right. Now, let me also add my e-mail passwords here. Now, let's combine it.

```
#define emailSenderAccount "eduengteamen@gmail.com"
#define emailSenderPassword "asm@496487"
#define emailRecipient "eduengteam@gmail.com"
#define smtpServer "smtp.gmail.com"
#define smtpServerPort 465
#define emailSubject "ESP32 Testing Email"

SMTPData smtpData;
```

```
Sketch uses 940210 bytes (71%) of program storage space. Maxim
Global variables use 40328 bytes (12%) of dynamic memory, leav
```

Okay, now done combining the next step is uploading the code to our yes people and see if the email is sent or not.

EXAMPLE CODE

```cpp
#include "ESP32_MailClient.h"

const char* ssid = "Ashraf TV ";

const char* password = "";

#define emailSenderAccount "eduengteamen@gmail.com"

#define emailSenderPassword ""

#define emailRecipient "eduengteam@gmail.com"

#define smtpServer "smtp.gmail.com"

#define smtpServerPort 465

#define emailSubject "ESP32 Testing Email"

SMTPData smtpData;

void setup() {

  // put your setup code here, to run once:

  WiFi.begin(ssid, password);

  while(WiFi.status() != WL_CONNECTED)

  {

  Serial.print("*");

  delay(200);

  }

  Serial.println("WiFi is Connected");

  smtpData.setLogin(smtpServer, smtpServerPort, emailSenderAccount, emailSenderPassword);
```

```
smtpData.setSender("ESP32 Sender", emailSenderAccount);

smtpData.setPriority("High");

smtpData.setSubject(emailSubject);

//smtpData.setMessage("Hellow World This is ESP Email Testing", false);

smtpData.setMessage("<div style=\"color:#2fffff;\"><h1>Hello</h1><p>-Sent from ESP32</p></div>", true);

smtpData.addRecipient(emailRecipient);

if(!MailClient.sendMail(smtpData))

 Serial.println("Error in Sending the Email" + MailClient.smtpErrorReason());

 smtpData.empty();

}

void loop() {

// put your main code here, to run repeatedly:

}

void sendCallback(SendStatus message)

{

Serial.println(message.info());


if(message.success()){Serial.print("++++++++");}

}
```

PRACTICAL TESTING

Now that I have hooked up my E.S.P ball. Let's go to the device manager to make sure that it can recognize the board. So boards a sunken fort.

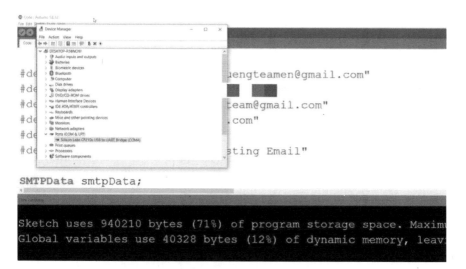

Let's go to the tools menu and make sure that we have everything right. Come for that. The E.S.P. Thirty-two difficult valiant one all everything's okay. And we have the code compiled. Now, let's upload a code. It will take a few seconds. For Arduino to upload the code Tor E.S.P board. OK. As you can see, applauding, he was sent up to, I think, 100 percent. OK, now, a hundred percent done. Applauding Now if we go here to our e-mail account and refresh. Let's open up to Reno and see CNN. Hey, listen. The moderate. What were the budgeteers? OK. We have a here.

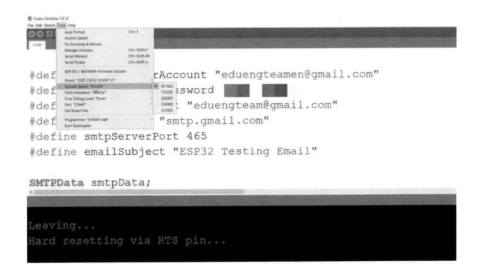

OK. We don't have this port right here. Now, this is the sender's e-mail account.

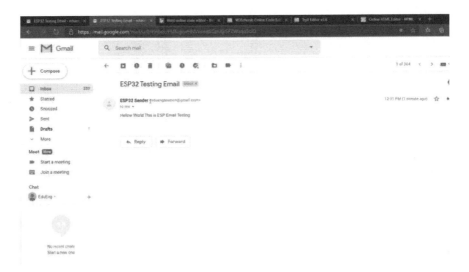

And as you can see, this message was sent from the sender's e-mail account, which is our account. Then you are proud that we created and we should receive that e-mail on our other account, which is lida, you, and GTM. That's it. We have a new e-mail. This is the new e-mail that we received from the sender whose which is named E.S.P 332 sender, and this is that a C recipient email. And we have this plain text message. Now we can adjust the code so that we can receive the Etchingham message.

We can uncomment these two and we can comment that plain text message. Then upload the code again. To receive an SDM, an encoded message. Okay, let's. Make them a shell of Cordin one line. That's right. Now upload again. OK. Now, as you can see here, we have a stream encoded message. This is the plain text message or the plain road text message. And this is Jim.

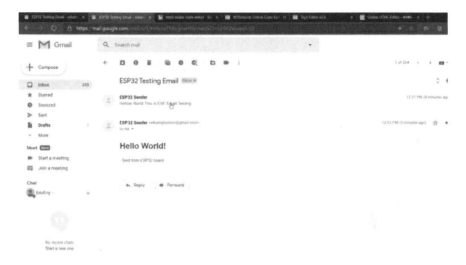

The encoded message that we did send using our E.S.P people. So if you want to send a plain text message, you have to pass the false value as a second parameter for the message, buddy. And if you want to send a jam and code, you need to paste to assemble code. Then through the second parameter for the empty B message Pardis send. That's it. This is how you can easily send e-mail messages from your U.S. people to your e-mail address, and we can configure this to send census data and any other type of information from E.S.P to our e-mail.

SENSOR ALERT VIA EMAIL

Now that we have sent an email, we can configure this email to include sensitive data. So what we need to do at this point is go back to our code. Let's save it. Let's call it called sense or e-mail.

```
Serial.println("WiFi is Connected");

smtpData.setLogin(smtpServer, smtpServerPort, emailSenderAccoun
smtpData.setSender("ESP32 Sender", emailSenderAccount);
smtpData.setPriority("High");
smtpData.setSubject(emailSubject);
//smtpData.setMessage("Hellow World This is ESP Email Testing",
smtpData.setMessage("<div style=\"color:#2fffff;\"><h1>Hello</1
```

```
Sketch uses 940242 bytes (71%) of program storage space. Maximu
Global variables use 40328 bytes (12%) of dynamic memory, leavi
```

Now we have this code that we can edit. What we need to do is to read that much since sort of at this point in our E.S.P board, you can use that template Charleson saw or any other type of sense, or just connect to the right pen. Now. The first thing that we need to do is create a new variable. Just make it integer and let's name it to touch value. Now, inside this method, we can. Into the loop. And take this variable that has such value inside the loop. And make it equal that its function and just assume that we are using that much sense for our PINfor now to give the reading, let's print it and see aromatherapy cereal print and. And let's print it out. The Dutch since so value.

```
void loop() {
  // put your main code here, to run repeatedly:
  touchValue = touchRead(4);
  Serial.print(The touch sensor value);
}
```

```
Sketch uses 940242 bytes (71%) of program storage space. Maximu
Global variables use 40328 bytes (12%) of dynamic memory, leavi
```

No. And not a politician. Okay, next, let's add Syria, not PLINT alone. And let's pass the torch value, okay? Now that we have the house value, we can't add a condition. If statement, you can choose the very same thing for temblors, Charleson, Salz, or any other type of sensor. Now let's say the touch value is above all, equal to 100. We need it to send us an email. And we need to send the message in this email to be. Let's do this. Let's go with this here. So we have the message to be. And plain text. Now, send the message. We need to write to the Dutch since so valuable. It's above a hundred now. We will receive an email stating this after receiving the email with a daily. Now, this may delay 1000 seconds, then we need to make this, which is make sure that we don't have any errors and. Add that faceplant. Scroll back here. Now, what will happen here? I will receive an email with this message once a sense of value is above 100. You can out of ten maliciousness or and if that sense of value is above 50, you can receive an email with an alert to make sure that, you know, there is High-temperature on the location and you can check it out. After that, we are adding that faceplant and we are sending that email with us and T.P data.

```
if(touchValue >= 100)
{
  smtpData.setMessage("The Touch Sensor value is above 100", tr
  smtpData.addRecipient(emailRecipient);

if(!MailClient.sendMail(smtpData))
   Serial.println("Error in Sending the Email" + MailClient.smt

  smtpData.empty();
```

```
Sketch uses 940242 bytes (71%) of program storage space. Maximu
Global variables use 40328 bytes (12%) of dynamic memory, leavi
```

Then we are printing this and the Syrian author of We Have an Arrow. Then we are emptying the gas MTBE. That's it. This is how you can send an email. Let's commend the section of our code. Now, Lister's this hour to make sure that it works, you can move all of these to that void loop section. So let's move them, let's call me all of this. And pasted above this line. Here.

```
void loop() {
    // put your main code here, to run repeatedly:
  smtpData.setLogin(smtpServer, smtpServerPort, emailSenderAccou
  smtpData.setSender("ESP32 Sender", emailSenderAccount);
  smtpData.setPriority("High");
  smtpData.setSubject(emailSubject);
  touchValue = touchRead(4);
  Serial.print("The touch sensor value: ");
```

```
Sketch uses 940242 bytes (71%) of program storage space. Maximu
Global variables use 40328 bytes (12%) of dynamic memory, leavi
```

Now we have the looming details. We have the e-mail they send out with the priority on the e-mail subject. We are reading the sense of value and you are printing this sort of value on the scene in a minute. Then we are checking if the same sort of value is above 100 or equal to 100. Then we are sending our message, an e-mail message. And let's comment on these parts from here. Add this to comment on it. OK, now let's verify the code, then upload it. Thought E.S.P that. I will hook up my ball to my E.S.P. OK, now they ask people what is hooked up. Now let's move on to now let's upload our code to the E.S.P board that we just connected to, make sure that we are receiving the same sort of data. Now. As you can see, the court is applauding and the balls connecting through come forth.

```
/*
if(!MailClient.sendMail(smtpData))
    Serial.println("Error in Sending the Email" + MailClient.smt

    smtpData.empty();*/
}

void loop() {
    // put your main code here, to run repeatedly:
```

```
Writing at 0x00070000... (75 %)
Writing at 0x00074000... (78 %)
Writing at 0x00078000... (81 %)
Writing at 0x0007c000... (84 %)
```

Now it's applauding that code to the E.S.P memory. Now, done uploading. That's it. Now. We need to make sure that we have. Since we're reading. Let's check that e-mail to make sure. OK. We are receiving on email. And as you can see, that much sense of value is above 100.

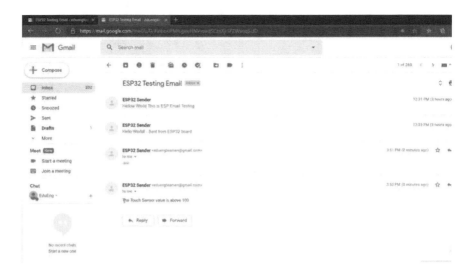

And I received the same email on my mobile phone. So the central value, in this case, is above 100. You can also send that sense of value on the email itself. It will be a very easy thing to do. But this is the main point, and we have a problem here. We received over 10 emails. This is because, in our code and the loop inside the whole function, we only added 1000, 1000 milliseconds, which is one second.

```
if(!MailClient.sendMail(smtpData))
    Serial.println("Error in Sending the Email" + MailClient.smt

    smtpData.empty();
delay(100000);
    }
}
```

```
Leaving...
Hard resetting via RTS pin...
```

So we will keep receiving emails every second. We can increase this number to be. Like 10 or 100 seconds, then we can't upload the code. OK, now what I did hear is I have seen that sentence, that much sense of value is above 100 blasts that much value. It will send that touchstone sort of value with that email. And I added a hundred seconds between every e-mail and the next one. So lists check to see. What we did receive.

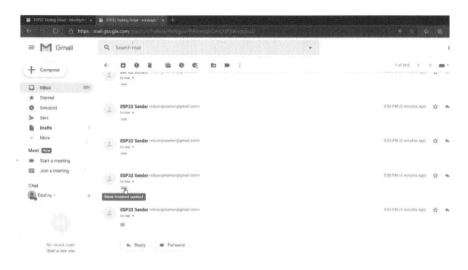

Now, as you can see here, we are receiving their sense of value. It's a 99. And we didn't get the line, which is the first sense of value above 100 because it's not above That's it. This is basically how easily you can send since all data are to your e-mail or how to get an email alert when the sense of value goes above a certain value.

CONTROLLED WITH A BUTTON

Now that we are done with the LED example, let's say it. And let's call it BLENKIN. Now let's create a new project. And as you can see in this project, we need to change the board. To E.S.P. And from here, you can select. I know these ESPN and we will go with the general one. Now, if you want to turn it on and off using a baton, let's say that the baton is connected to be number two and we want to control a that is connected to the number three or vice versa, to say that that it is connected to number two and the baton is connected to number three, the output. Of this baton. Must be sent as that digital input for this spin that has delayed so as you can see here, the output of that general-purpose input-output

PINthree will be sent to the input of the digital PINtwo. So if this is on, it will turn on the two. If it is off. It will turn off the print on number two. Now, the input to this pin, which is then our purpose, input-output, PINthree will be the button. So the button will send five volts or ground and the output will be five volts or ground. This output will turn on. All of that is connected to number two. And this is basically how easy it is to control pain or control added using a button. So when you connect a button, you just need to upload this call to your E.S.P board. And whenever you click on the button that's connected to the number three, it will turn on the lid on PINtwo. And as you can see, I only connected one line. I haven't, uh, coded anything. You don't have to write anything and everything will work just fine. Thanks for this one. This is an example. Let's save it button. Let's control the example.

UPLOAD BUTTON CODE AND TEST IT

Now let's upload the new code to our E.S.P board and test out the button connection and for easier access, since we have defaulted on our breadboard visible and easier to connect, we are going to change this. Disconnect this link and we are going to connect general-purpose and output to the input of the digital pen that has the built and led, which is the real purpose and what output. Number two, now save your work and click on the Arduino Idy. And this is basically what we are going to do. We are going to connect a button which now, which is in our case our two PINPINfour, and this button will control the and turn it on and off. So let's upload the code. We have the right configurations, so click on onto. Both baton. Now it's uploading. Done uploading now when we click here. As you can see, the lid is on, let's connect using our let's connect digital PINfour to five volts or grams. So using this simple wire we can do is the following. Now we have this wire connected to the general-purpose and put out a PINfor what we need to do now is to connect five vaults or ground. So here we have a ground pin. So once you select or connect this to the ground beneath that, it will turn off. Now, when you connect it to five vaults or when you release it, it will turn on again when you connect to the ground that it will turn on. And when you connect it to five vaults, then it will turn on. Now, that's it. This is basically how you can connect a baton and control Alade using the urinal without writing a single code, I used a wire and you can replace the wire with a tinkle on the resistor and a button, either in the pull-up or pull downstate. It can work both ways, but this is the main concept.

PRACTICAL EXAMPLE INFRARED OBSTACLE AVOIDANCE SENSOR

Now we are going to take the knowledge that we have so far. To make a project or an in-flight obstacle, avoiding avoidance project, is the sense that we are going to use now. These are small sensors that are often used in robots. The infrared sensor works by sending an infrared light,

using this sled with some frequency and then detecting if some of the light has reflected the receiver here, the most common ones have a digital output indicating if the object has been detected, many of them have the option to be enabled or disabled in this section. I will show you how easy it is to connect and use such a sensor with your esport. Some of the sensors have a brief detection when they are enabled and in this section, I will also show you how you can suppress this false detection with visual. Now. What you need is this sensor module and it comes in two types, three pens, and four pens, the three print versions cannot be enabled or disabled, while the Forbin version that we have here has an optionally enabled pen, which is this pen, the fourth pen. And here I will use and describe the Forbin version that I have, and the information should also be relevant to other versions of the sensor. Now the infrared obstacle avoidance sensor has power, ground output, spin, or signal, which is the third one, and the Bilpin. There are also two potential meters and one Jumba, as you can see here. The first potential meter is used to adjust how sensitive the sensor is, you can use it to adjust the distance from the object at which the sensor detects signals. The second potential meter usually should not be changed, and it controls the frequency of the infrared signal. And is pleasant with a good sitting, so you don't need to change it. You may have or you may need to use it if there is any interference with other inside sources, otherwise, avoid changing it. If the enable pin of the board is not connected, the chamber should be placed on the board. As in this picture, the JUMBA permanently enables the board. And if the jumper is placed then a Bilpin, which is this pen, the fourth one cannot be used to enable or disable this board now. And the next lesson I will show you how you can easily connect this sensor in practice to your E.S.P ball and we will start testing this out.

LED BAR COUNTER ENCODER SHIFT REGISTER

we are going to introduce more advanced stuff like led bars, shift registers, rotary, and digital encoders and counters. Now, the knowledge that we will offer in this lesson can be applied to any microcontroller that you are using, whether it's Arduino E.S.P Penguin or a Raspberry Pi, or any other type of microcontroller. Now, to get things started, if you haven't already, you need to open up your visual software by going to the Start menu and selecting visual. Now, once you're on the software, you can see that here we have. The main area has a microcontroller.

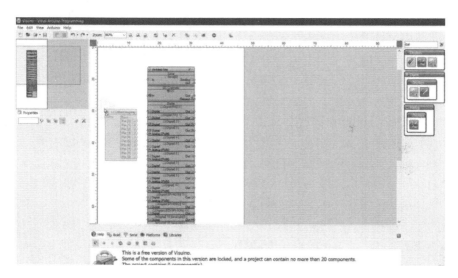

Let's start by adding a little bar so you can click this play and drag this little bar and display it to your design area or. You can simply go to the search box and write, but as you can see, we also have Dalbar. Now, the is a physical component that has more than one lead, depending on the one that you have, you might have nine, 10, or 11 levels. Now, if you want to increase the number of lids here to assist them with your bar, you can simply drag. And as you can see now, we have twenty-one being lit bar. We can go back to nine and vice versa. Now let's make it 10.

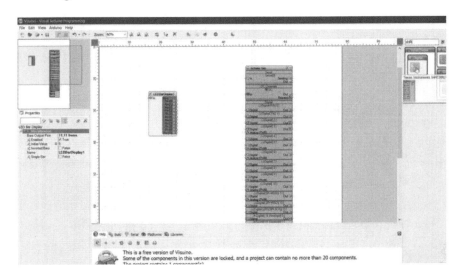

Now we need to control this border using a shift register so this little bot will be connected to the register and the shift register will be connected to are doing so here and right shift. Now, once you start a shift, you can see that we have a lock here. So let's track the shift register. Right here and at the end of this lesson, I will show you how you can activate a trial, let's say a trial period to this of the software, and remove this lock to use or to generate the Arduino code. But let's finish the connection first. Now, the shift just will minimize the number of pins that we need to use to control this little bar. But this bar is controlled using a rotary encoder like a potential meter. So to reach the rotor encoder, we need to write in code right here. And once we have here, we need to select Rotary encoders, and so as you can see here, we have a daughter, encoders and so in the digital section. So grab it and drop it here.

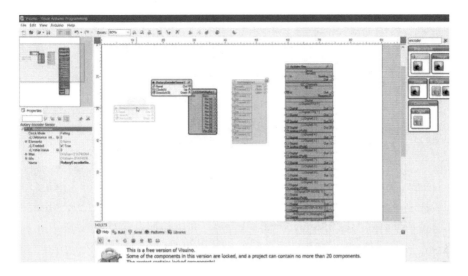

This is our rotary encoders. Now, this rotary encoders sensor has its pin o'clock in a direction for the rotation, clockwise or counterclockwise, and an output for the pulse up and down, plus the main rotary encoder output, which is a number that we will use to control the. But now the number that the encoder will give us cannot be sent directly to the bar. And to send directly to the to control which pins are turned on or off, we need to use a counter. And in this case, we need an up-down counter. So right counter. And as you can see here, we have more than one counter. This is a normal counter. This is an up-down counter. So grab it. Drop it here.

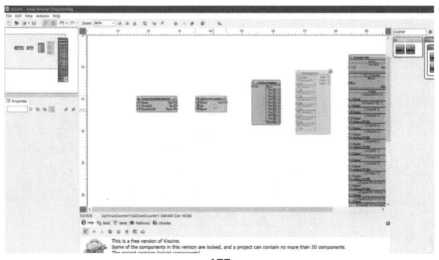

Now we have everything ready, the rotating encoder will send an output to the counter, which will turn this output into an Allitt pattern that will turn these lights on or off. And all of this is controlled using Arduino. Now, the first thing that we need to do is connect these items. We need to connect the output of the counter to the input of the lead, but we need to connect the USB with the amp here. And the down or the down here to make sure that they are in sync. Now we have a clock and direction pens and these two pens need to be connected to our Arduino board. We can connect the clock, Ben-To PINsix on our Arduino. And we can also pay we can also connect the direction pin to PINseven on our Arduino. Now we need to connect the lead bar and the shifters are together and we need to connect the shift just last hour arguing about. Now let's connect the shift, register the data. Been with PIN10. Now, you know. And the clock pins with PINnine. The large pin with PINeight.

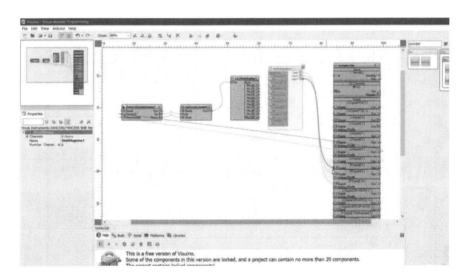

Now, you need to make sure that these connections match the physical connection that you have now. We need to connect these pins bar. Together with the Shifta Serpens. And to do so, we can simply drag and drop, let's leave the first pin, which has been zero and start connecting from PIN one.

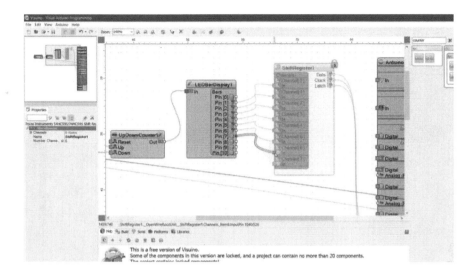

OK, now we need more items on this Shifter's Stuff channel, and to add more items, we need to unlock it first. Now, as you can see, here is a list of the items that you can use and you can't use now for this item.

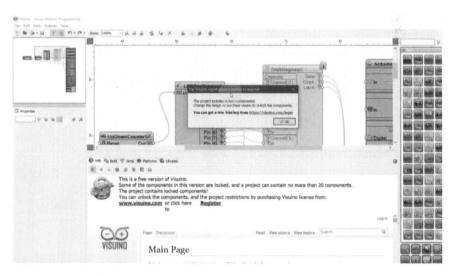

If you click here, you can see that the visual, just a registration is invalid or expired and you can get a free trial key by clicking here.

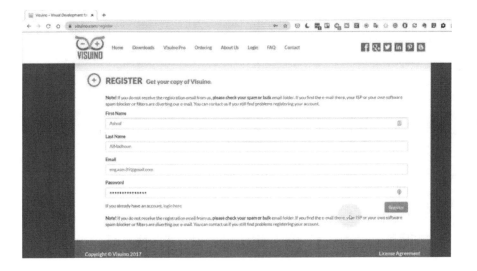

 Now, once you click here, you can simply go and click register here, fill in your information and your email address and write a password, then click register. Now, once you click register, you will receive an email. From. Vaginal and you need to activate your account using this email. Now, you will see the special need to confirm your email address to log on once you confirm your email address, by going to your email inbox and click on the link that you receive from know, you need to click, login and login using your username or email and password. Now, as you can see, your account or e-mail does not exist in our system because we haven't yet confirmed our email.

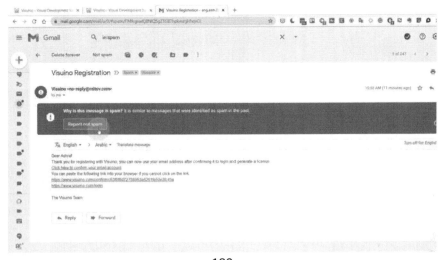

Now, usually, you will find a visual registration email in the spam folder, so you need to go to your email and make sure that you check the spam folder to see their email. Click once on the confirmed link and report, not spam.

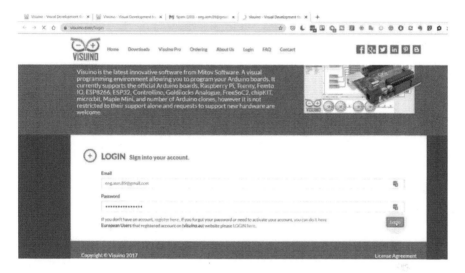

So that they can or you can receive new emails right to your inbox now, once you confirm, you can easily log on. To their website now, as you can see, we have a 15 or 15 yes, the 15-day trial lasted for zero dollars and you can generate that take.

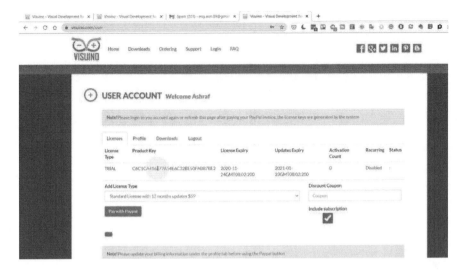

Now, once you generate it, as you can see, it will be valid for 13 days. You need to copy this key. Go back here. And simply.

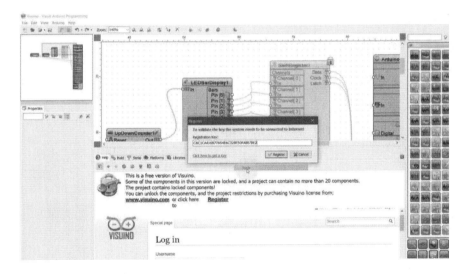

Click register places Europea click register again, click OK to start using visual, as you can see, you are running 15 days trial version of which we know you can purchase a full version. OK, now Schifter just starts to be usable. What you need to do next is simple.

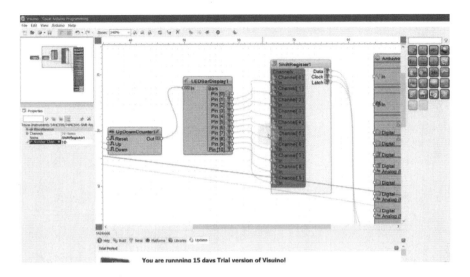

As you can see, this is the shift register and we need 10 channels, so change this to 10. Now proceed, connecting the components. That's it. Now we have our shifter's starlit Barbancourt encounter caught up and ready without writing a single code. Now let's zoom out to see the full design. Let's save it. The bar counter and encoder chef. First. Now, if you picked it here, it will send you to Arduino E, where you can get the code, which you can upload your Arduino board and use, but you need to make sure that you connect your circuit in the very same way.

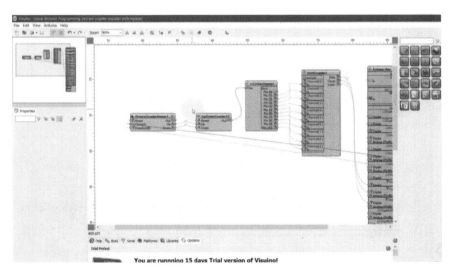

Now you need to have your lead power supply and a shift that you need to connect them. And you can need to connect that shifter start to yours. The microcontroller on our case, Arduino, and you need to connect the router, encoder clock, and Direxion pins to your microcontroller. That's it. These elements double down the counter and the encoder is software elements and a sort of coding. So you can easily implement this code.

TORQUE DESIGN CONCEPTS

So the first concept is about to talk about what it is. So let's first take a look at things that we do in our daily life. For example, if we have a tie here and we have some sort of French connected to the middle point of their diet and the length of the range is like this, or you can think of this circle like a door lock on the handle of the door when we push it down and open the door by pushing the door backward. The thing is, if we push this point in the downward direction, let's say it's a range. Let's stick to that example. What happens? This rod comes to this point, OK, after we push it downwards, what happens in the result? This nut or anything on which we are applying force is going to rotate, OK? And that is going to be a result. Or we would say that it is going to rotate whenever we go from this point to this point, that is the result we obtain after applying a force perpendicular to an axis. OK, I know these lines are very complicated, but we have to understand them to understand the concept of talk. But the interesting thing is if we extend this line or this length of the rod, we double it. We have to apply a little less force, as we all should know this by applying a force away from the point it is going to cost us less force. OK, so at this point, let's say I was pushing with one kg of fluid, or let's not confuse it, one kg of force. So if we extend the handle, I need to apply one point five force. OK, I'm just giving you an intuition. We can have the same results with less force, but we have to extend the length of the thing that we are applying force on. So this is a very important concept that is going to be used in the definition of talk. Now, what is dark is a perpendicular action. This is the perpendicular action and to which thing it is perpendicular to this point. It is perpendicular. OK, a 90 degree, OK, it is perpendicular action acting upon an axis. This is the axis. From a distance, this is the definition of dark and the distance is this green line, let's say it is 10 centimeters. So dark is a force, a result that is perpendicular to the axis from a distance. To appoint everything is concerning this point. So this is the definition of the dark. Now, let's understand it more intuitively. Let's say this is a door. OK. And we have the lock of this door at this point on both sides, OK, obviously, so we rotated and we pushed the door backward, I. Through this action, we would need to apply a certain force to push the door backward, and let's say after that, the door comes at this point so often rotating, obviously the lock and then pushing the door. That's one condition. Now, the second thing that I want to emphasize is if we have the lock at this point. And we rotated and then pushed the door backward in the second condition. Our force is going to be much more limited if it is F1 and F2, then if one is going to be less than two, OK, because it is a black eyeless distance from the point it is rotating. This is the point. It is rotating. And the distance here, let's say it is due to it, is less than the point here at one. So this one is greater than the two. And when the distance is greater, we have to apply less force to appoint around which we are rotating an object. That is the concept of torque and why I am taking a lot of time to explain it, because robotic arms used this concept to move the joints in all of the robotics, obviously where actuators are odd, we have to take into consideration the concept of thought to have a rotation to force and to select the motor. Even we have to consider the concept of. Now, in robotic arms, let's say this is a robotic arm. This is the point where a motor is connected, a joint, and at this point joint and a motor is connected, let's see. So how much does this motor requires and how much dark this motor requires is the question that I will be answering to the concept of thought? Let's say this is the point where one kg of anything, a brake or a mobile phone led to this much heavy is connected and the robot needs to hold it. If the dark is not enough in the motors, what will happen? It will fall to a certain point where the robot can handle not with the motors, just with the structure. OK, so we have to select the motors according to our requirement, for example, holding this mobile phone in it to a certain point in X, Y, Z, we then select these motors depending upon the torque required.

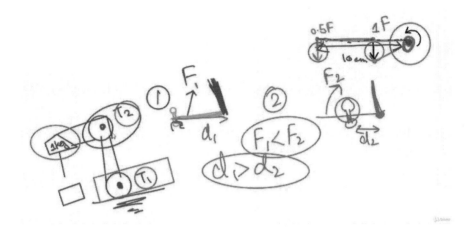

So it is a very important concept, especially for robotic arms. So let's now move to the next.

Selection Components for the Design

So let's move on to the motor selection, a proper understanding of how we are going to select the motor. This is our D.C. motor that we are going to be using. And like all these motors, you just apply the power to the motors with two connectors and it starts to rotate. This is how we are going to be using our DC motor that is coupled with the tire. This is the gear said. This is the DC motor and it is copied here. And Alberca connects the motor to the body of the robot talking about the speed of the robot. If we supply convoys and one beer, this diet is going to revolve 140 times in a minute. OK, that is quite a decent speed and that's how electric motor speeds are admired currently at this point where the tide is gapper is the point where force is applied.

When we move the robot at the very starting point of the shaft of the motor is going to the maximum. That is seven point five. The stalled talk of this motor then applied toward and won a bit. Now, if we extend the shaft and connect it at this point, let's say it is 15 millimeters that torque the Stalter, the maximum torque is going to get is OK. It becomes five kilograms. And that's how the relation is the maximum distance between the point with the maximum motor have and the point at which node is placed, the talks decreases. iRobot robot is not going to be a vidro word, OK, so it is going to be operating on a DC battery and that is going to be a light bulb. Let's take a look at your specs.

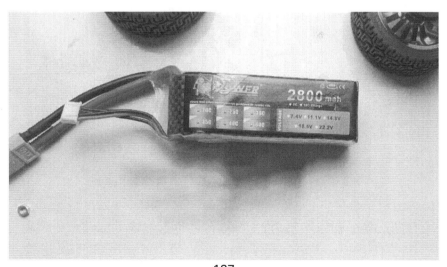

Since our battery, which is 20 800 mph battery, which means two point eight amperes are well, this is about current, but what about the voltage? These three cells represent the voltage, which each cell is three-point seven volts when fully charged. OK, so which is round about near 212 volts, which is our requirement. So talking about the power requirement of our system is Robonaut two motors requiring 12 Volt and two Embiid for both of them one on one and before both the motors and very little amount of current for a microcontroller motor driver to run and we will be adding some sensors that will also require five volts and a very minimal amount of current major power consumption. Things are motor and this battery we can run both of the motors at maximum speeds of there for one complete are and still, we would be having eight hundred million extra. So in other words, it is going to work for us for a longer period because we would not be using the motors at full speed all the time. The brain of a human being is the main thing. So same goes for the robot microcontroller is known as the brain of the robot. And for our level of understanding, the microcontroller is working as the main processor or key. The first comparison, E.S.P, 32 years to six is Wi-Fi compatible. Nano does not support Wi-Fi.

So we are not going to deal with our Nano or Uuno now compared to the 66 and 32 comparisons. Both are good, but 86 takes a single core and 32 is dual-core. But in simple words, E.S.P 32 is the successor of eight to six and it is dueled. And the power of these characteristics is taken into consideration when there is a lot of communication happening, some serious communication with Allport, or all registers are utilized. But in our case, things are going to be not that complicated. So we are going to simply select E.S.P 32. As a reporter says, electrical knowledge is required a bit, but still, you need to understand how to connect the modules and how to supply a required amount of power to the respective modules. So we have to understand how to do the electrical connections. Let's take a look. This is our motor driver. And why do we need it? Because motors are going to be consuming a huge amount of power, electrical power, as compared to the microcontroller and the sensors that you will be going to be using in future projects. But the thing is, we have to isolate and supply proper electrical power to the motors and not make that power come into the microcontroller because the microcontroller work at five volts and some amps, some hundred million, whereas the motor that working at Ambient proper amperes if somehow that electrical power went into the bot towards the microcontroller, it will burn to make things easy. Let's raise them and perform some electrical connections that we will be going to be doing in real-time.

But first, we need to understand what is going to be the connections microcontroller is going to be using to Binz to control the direction of a single motor.

So in our case, we need four for that purpose. And after some time we will be discussing GWM and for that, we need one extra pane of the microcontroller that is going to be connected to the motor driver for speed control battery is going to be supplied directly to the motor driver and this motor driver is going to output or somehow electrically downgrade the power from 12 to Five-fold and it is going to be supplying a microcontroller and future coming sensors after understanding this. One thing is remaining before we build the robot, and that is the structure. Let's take a look. We understood all the modules, right, and electrical connections as well. Now it's time to understand how we are going to stack them up or arrange them in a structure to design a body. OK, this is going to be the basic structure of holding our motors. And frankly, we have to design such a thing that will carry all of these things. After that, we are going to be placing the battery between these things and then the microcontroller. Now, as we are going to be 3D printing, let's take the measurements where we will do the holes in our bodies.

UNDERSTANDING ELECTRONIC SUPPLY

Now, what is going to be electronics? We are going a bit practical now. So the first and important thing that I have selected is nine nine six are M.G. servo motor.

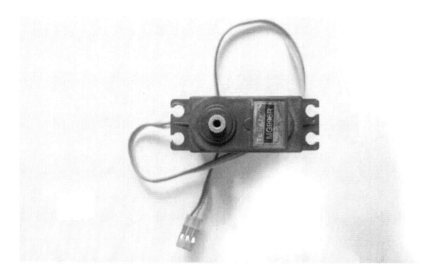

This servo motor has eleven points five, I guess KG's Berson Demetre of Torque.

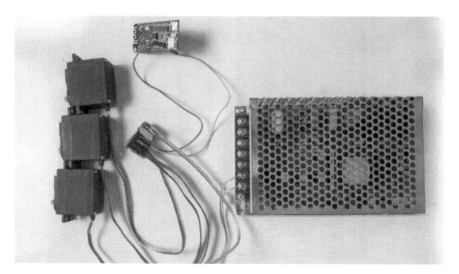

OK, now what this eleven point five kilograms or centimeter means that if we apply. From one centimeter distance, a force from we rotate this mortar and this the right moves. This is the concept of the target with respect, it can move 11 kilograms of load. OK, so what happens? If we extend this distance to two centimeters and at this point, it is two centimeters, how much maximum load this motors at full rated voltage and current it can move, it is going to be 5.5 kilograms. So what happened? The total torque gets divided by the distance of half on the road. So if the next joint is connected at this point, this motor is going to be able to carry only 5.5 kilograms. is again a lot. And if you see the distance we have in our joints is ten point seven centimeters and stuff like that. So dark gets reduced with a very huge margin. But still, the calculations we will be doing after this electronics understanding is going to tell us about how I selected this motor. OK, the electronics that we are going to be using is this simple and basic connection. Now, this seems to be a bit of not a robotic thing, but this is going to be the actual connectivity in a robot. And what it is, this is a 220 to the five-volt power supply. We supply 220 the AC supply to this and it produces five volts, positive five volts and groaned at these two points. One, Edison wanted this. What happens? Five Volt is going to be supplied at this point. Now, this is a real this is interesting

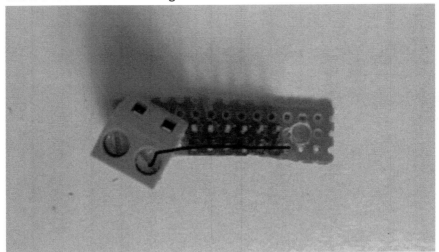

What is happening point to this point, everything is connected in cities. And again, from this point to all of these points, these are connected. If I supply five volts here, all of these white bins are going to have five votes, but not the black one. If I supply six votes here, then Six-fold is going to be applied to only Deed's in a line, not to these white ones. OK, that is what I call a series read. So why do I need that? If you take a look in the servo motor, it is going to be requiring a ground, a signal, and one another thing, a five-fold connection. Six. Sorry, but I will be providing five points five with this power supply. And the thing is, these all turbo motors. We have four servo motors running the claw as well. That is going to be connected to a rail because they have a common connection of ground and six Fords. That's why I've connected them in CCDs at this point. And this microcontroller also requires five and ground to all of these are connected to the source of the power supply that we have. One important thing here is the power supply must supply five volts to six words in between any words of six words. But the important thing is each of these servo motors at maximum load that we are going to push them to is going to require one and fear each motor, which is one, two, three, three, and four years in total. And your power supply should be capable enough to do that. I tried to supply it with a mobile phone charger. It was only capable of supplying one point five beers to improve. Was written to my motors, were not properly responding me. They were stuttering or producing certain undesirable results. This is the connectivity. All of these servo motors are supplied ground. Then five words and the signal wires are going to be connected from each. Ben, that we will select each of these servo motors, OK? Currently, they are not connected. We'll look at it in detail. So that is the electronics that we are going to be using. And now let's take a look at your calculator.

CALCULATING REQUIRED TORQUE FOR MOTORS

So what is going to be our total target requirement? OK, this is a very important question for our robotic arm design. So what we are going to do is take a look at this website.

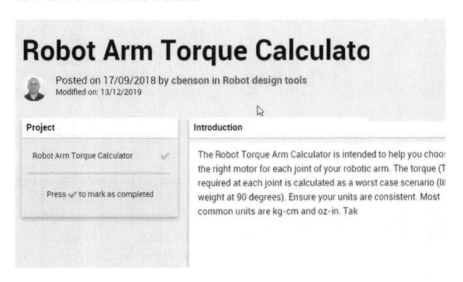

That is the robotic robot shark dot com, and that has a robot arm calculated by Stephensen. And you can Google it easily and try to provide the link as well. So what it does is it gives the design a reference image so you can place the values of your robot or your design in it and it can tell you about the target requirements. So I have given the values that our robot is going to have, which is two point one nine centimeters. Of this 11 link that is going to be from the last joint to the blog, Magal Point. OK, and what weight it is going to have, it is going to be having five grams, only the 3D plastic weight that is going to be having after that. The main thing about the robot design is how much load it is going to carry. So currently I have said 400 grams, OK, everything is engaged, so I have to write zero points for it. Said the Last motor that you are going to be using should have this much torque.

- **A1**: can represent the load being lifted.

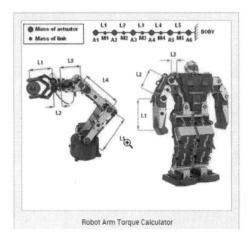

Robot Arm Torque Calculator

OK, kg centimeter after that it said what is going to be the link to value. We don't have a link to we have link number three and actually, we have three degrees of freedom Roubaud. So we have only three motors for actuation, three lengths, three joints, and the last motor is actually for only the plant.

L: [cm]	M: [kg]	A: [kg]	I: [kg cm]
L1: 2.19	M1: 0.005	A1: 0.4	T1: 0.881475
L2: 0	M2: 0	A2: 0	T2: 0
L3: 8.33	M3: 0.005	A3: 0.055	T3: 4.734100000(
L4: 10.43	M4: 0.005	A4: 0.055	T4: 10.18377500(
L5: 10.43	M5: 0.005	A5: 0.055	T5: 16.25924999¢
L6: 0	M6: 0	A6: 0	T6: 0

OK, similarly, we provided the values that we have on the linked number three linked number for the length of a robotic arm that we will see when we will be designing it. Then the masses, these masses are the 3D plastic mass and I have written five grams for each, although one was having four rounds and one was having six times over that and five grams for each weight of the actuators. I have used the same motors, nine, nine, six, or seven soldiers, all have fifty-five grams of read-only, but they provide a huge amount of thought. Now, this is an interesting thing. What is going to be the target requirement of Ford Motors, it is. It is saying that we need four point seven kg per centimeter and this motor attached at L3 is going to have 11 kilograms. OK? Similarly, Ford Motor is ten points one. How much thought is required as compared to the previous one? Similarly to the next point, the joint motor, which is the last motor that is going to be the main base motor that will take the whole robot requires sixteen point two kilograms per centimeter of torque, although our motor cannot supply that much, according to the datasheet. But I have rotated the robot and it is moving easily. But the thing is, I have not placed this amount of load at the end effector. OK, so if I increase it, let's say one kg of holding torque is required by the robotic arm. Let's take a look at the requirements of the task for the motors. It is increased to 11 22 kg and 35 kilograms for the base motor. So this robot calculator is interesting to find the amount of talk that we need for our robot.

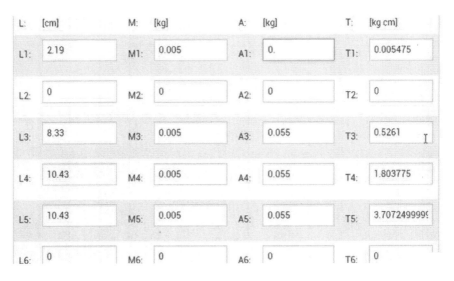

L:	[cm]	M:	[kg]	A:	[kg]	T:	[kg cm]
L1:	2.19	M1:	0.005	A1:	0.	T1:	0.005475
L2:	0	M2:	0	A2:	0	T2:	0
L3:	8.33	M3:	0.005	A3:	0.055	T3:	0.5261
L4:	10.43	M4:	0.005	A4:	0.055	T4:	1.803775
L5:	10.43	M5:	0.005	A5:	0.055	T5:	3.7072499999
L6:	0	M6:	0	A6:	0	T6:	0

So we will stick to zero point three or zero point four is good. Let's say 100 grams is good, we'll go with it. Or obviously, our object is going to be very much less than four hundred. But for just a reference, this table is good to find the talk for our robotic arm. So let's start designing it and understand the concept that I want to give you.

ROBOTIC ARM THEORETICAL UNDERSTANDING

To design a robotic arm first, we need to develop some concepts about different types of robotic arms and the design of our robot that will be following a certain type of robotic arms type that is going to be a gene manipulator, anthropomorphic gene manipulator, or serial manipulator. Let's take a look here.

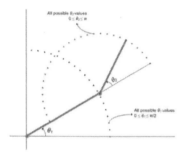 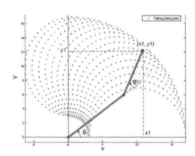

And there are three main jargons that I would be using throughout this project from now on. And those are going to be gene manipulators and or you can see to be a serial manipulator. OK, and it is going to be following this symmetry, this structure, one joint here, one joint here, and another joint at this point. This is known as serial linked joint serial linked actuators and links in between them. This blue line is the link, OK, and these circles, the actuators, the motors, General Motors are known as Joint One Joint Connect BlueLinx. This is the theory behind Link and join. The next thing that comes into question is what are the spaces for our robotic arm? Ask space and workspace. This is a two-joint manipulator, a serial manipulator, which has a task base, let's say, to draw an arc. OK, this is going to be its task. So this is its task space, a space in which the robotic arm has to perform a task. This task space is a subspace of the whole workspace. That robotic arm can perform. If this joint if we rotate this joint, what happens? The dotted form and at this point. So there are limits obviously to each of the germs. It cannot rotate 60 in all directions. There are physical limits or several motors that we have move only to 180 degrees. And again, if we move this joint too, let's say, to 90 degrees, what will happen, it will come at this point. And the link, this second joint is going to be at this point later. So, again, it can rotate and move and draw these points. What this dotted line they represent is. The workspace of this robotic arm, specifically the two joint serial manipulators, what is workspace is the total possible movement of the anger factor of our robotic arm in a 3D space or 2D space representation, which is this all of the points that are presented in X and Y, these two images are obtained from the networks and they're good for the representation of workspace and tasks. That space is not represented here. What I do to give you an example through this task, and obviously, it is just to deal with a robotic arm, so its space is to deal f OK in 2D, it can be drawn in 3D and it can be increased by adding several joints and degrees of freedom increases to what is going to be a basic design. We are going to have. A simple. Link the first link in the Z-axis, if we draw all of this axis here like this, this is the Z says, this is why X and this is the X-axis. So what happens is first we draw the Z-axis. After that, we are going to have another link in the X Y-axis that is going to be on the right side of the left side. It can be connected in both axes. I am going to say anything that is not Z and I'm going to see it in the X and Y. So this is going to be a link. Then again, we are going to have a joint at this point, which is going to be a servo motor. And at this point, we are also going to have one. We are going to also have one here. Now, from this point, we are again going to have a link here and then we are going to have a servo motor at this point. And again, it is going to be connected to a clock. OK, a clock is going to be like this. I'm trying to draw it a little better, but I don't think so. It is happening. So it is going to be like this, a clock, the distance that I am assuming it to have ten point seven centimeters here, ten-point four centimeters or seven centimeters, same distance at this point in centimeters. And this one is going to be, I guess, 11 centimeters. These are going to be drawn in such a way to develop a gear that when the motor rotates the cerebral motor, the claws close and open, according to the movement of the seven or so sort of a gear assembly is going to be utilized.

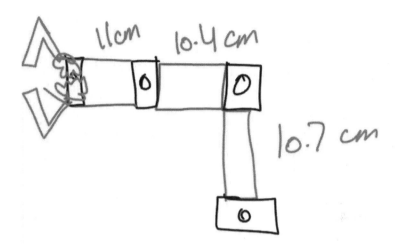

This is going to be the basic design of a robotic arm. I'll add certain good-looking features to a robotic arm. But the thing important here is I am going to make it a not efficient design because I want to represent you. The basic things that are required to make the motors whole in the 3D space and the wiring are not going to be looking good because I have not heard anything about how I will erase the wires and what the circuit is going to be. So wires are going to be outside here on the body and there will be a lot of wires for you to remove the connection wires and power supply wires. So it is not going to be looking good, but still. We have to design the basic robotic arm to get started. So let's jump into Fusion 360 and start designing it, then 3-D printing it.

3D MODELING AND BUILDING THE ROBOT

From mobile robotics, I guess you have a bit of an idea about Fusion 360. I am not going to start drawing pricing sea to start a circle at certain axes that I select.

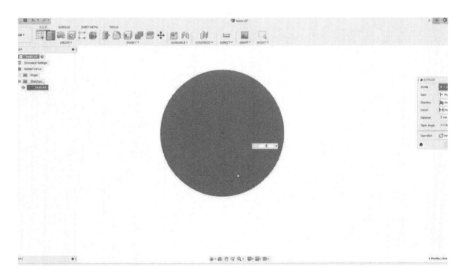

And this circle is going to be a 53 radius, obviously, but it is going to be the base circle, the base length circle. And I will be kept on trying things. I have first created the design on paper and then I started designing how my robot should look like. And I have some skills in Fusion 360. And if you want to learn Fusion 360, there are a lot of tutorials available I keep on drawing. The drawing is not a sort of solution code. You can just take a look at it and draw it yourself or understand how you can design.

The important step is where we have to import the Servo Motor 996 3D model into our design to consider it to make it visually easy to understand. If replace the servo motor at a certain point, then what will happen and how our design will work or how we will be designing a robot with the help of 3D models of every company.

Servo motor is an important one. And again, I will import the servo motor for my reference to make my design accurate and I will bring the horrible motor to a specific position and then start drawing the next link. You can see this is the basic design of our robotic arm that we will be using with three several motors.

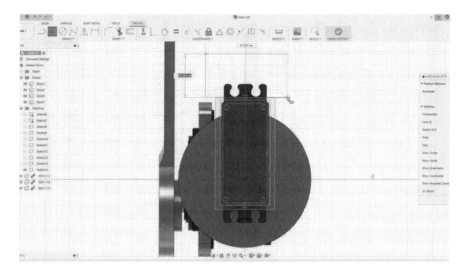

One important thing is left, and that is the base, how we are going to connect the base to something stiff enough to hold the whole robotic arm. And regarding the claw, multiple claws are available online.

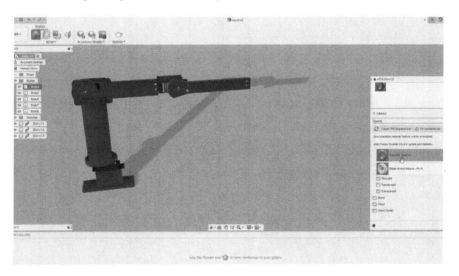

You can download them or make your own Glawe. Mikola is not that strong. So I would recommend you to make your own Glawe animated and take a look at its final look.

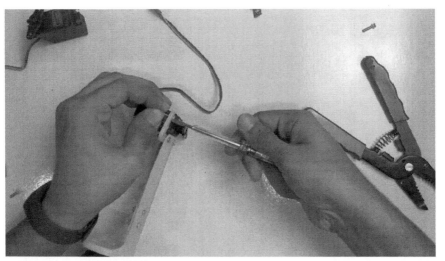
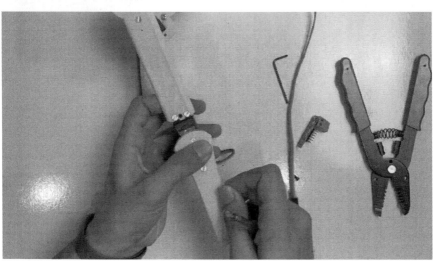

TESTING SERVO MOTORS

I board looks beautiful, right? Let's open up the fetal monitor and first give the signal to the first several more pressing.

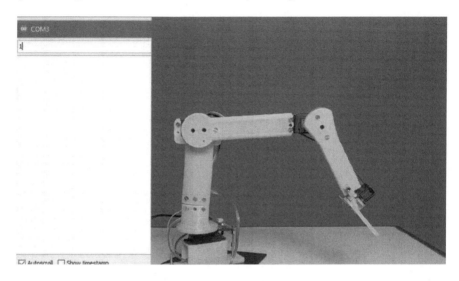

And did we send the signal the robot did not even move? The reason is our robot is not connected with the same signal again sent. Still, the robot is not moving because our robot is not connected to the power supply. Now we connected it a sort of just happened. Now we are going to give the signal. You have to look at the first servo motor the clock. It opened, right? So it was not appearing. rotating this second servo motor, this servo motor is going to make the whole robot move because it is the base motor. This 90-degree motion produced the whole robot to rotate. You can see the wires, the ugly wires. The thing is, the structure is not that stiff and that causes a lot of problems. You can see the movement of the robot with the servo angle is accurately moving, but the structure is so fragile that it keeps shaking for discourse one on one. This robotic arm is good, but for Professor Cooper says, I will not be using or not even considering such kind of design. OK, this is the simplest design you can do.

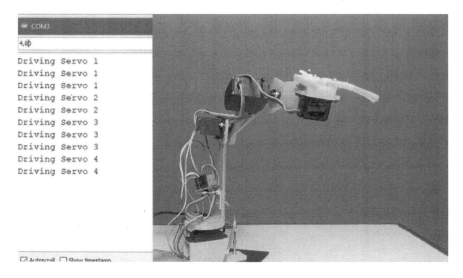

We can simplify it as well. We are now going to give the command to the fourth servo motor to rotate fourteen hundred degrees, OK, making a 140 and this is the time to make that law close.

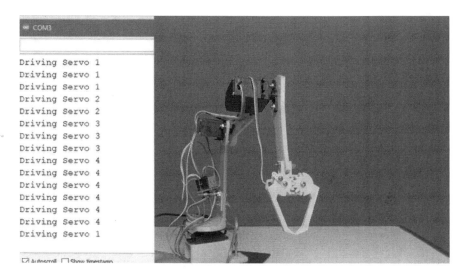

OK, so the first motor is 30 degrees and the clock gets close sort of obtaining the object or gripping the object.

UNDERSTANDING PICK AND PLACE BEHAVIOR

Our robot is ready and you can see it right here holding the mic. The purpose I made it for. Just joking. Now we are going to do the first practical thing with the robotic arm, and that is to pick an object rotated and drop the object at a certain point. And it can repeat this behavior. But for the robotic one or one, this action is good and I call it lame. But remember, this is not the proper way we deal with robotic arms. But for the robotic arm project one on one, this is going to be the first step that we will take. Why? I call it lame because this is a robotic arm and we have joints. Then we have a claw at the end like this. OK. Joined here, joined here, joined here and joined here now what I will be going to do is rotate the load, said this joint to 40 degrees. And the anger factor is going to be at this point, let's say it is going to pick the object like this by rotating this joint, which is going to be at this point to go to zero dark thirty degrees and it will close itself to hold the object. Then we will rotate this joint to I guess it is going to be 60 degrees and the whole robot will be rotated and it will come to like this and the clock will be at this point. Then we again rotate this joint to 40 degrees and it will then point towards this point and we will open the claw to drop the object so the robot can repeat the behavior.

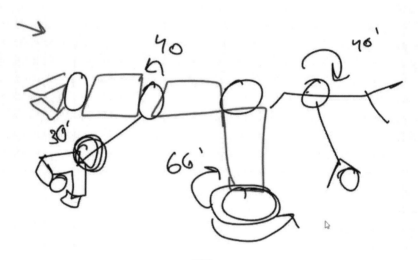

And we are going to do it with the scientific thing that is known as delays. If you have taken the project of mobile robotics, it would be called hour delays, giving delays and using them in your programs, a good quality project. So what is going to be the flow of our code? I recommend you if you haven't taken the mobile robotics one on one, you should take that because I have explained the code from the very basic. But now I'm not going to go into detail about the functions of the Arduino idea. I'm just going to say the first function is going to be to move the robot, then give a delay, then move the third joint and again move the first move, the first joint and third joint, then delay. And then I would say draw the required object like this. These are going to be function calls similar to this. And a robotic behavior is going to be achieved that we want to do with the robot. It will play big, the object rotated, drop it on another location. It will go back to the point where it can grab the object and then go back to the point where it dropped the previous one. So that is going to be the thing. But the interesting thing is we are going to be doing it with delays. And that's why I call it a lame project as the robot does not know what is the exact position of its end effect, that that is the thing that is required in a lot of applications. What is the point with your endpoint is the robot will be so dumb that it will not be doing anything about its pull and effector's location. It is just going to be rotating, giving a delay, then picking the object, then giving a delay, and dropping the object. That is just going to be the process. And one important thing, the robot is going to be moving so fast that it is going to be almost breaking its sporty. So let's take a look at the code.

PROGRAMMING PICK AND THROW

This court is interesting, its output is even more interesting, the thing is, I tried my best to make the robot hold the object and drop it in a proper place, but because of the speed of the servo motors, that is not being controlled. The robot was throwing the objects away and it was making me angry. Yes, but let's learn it first, and then we will optimize it, OK?

```
1b_Object_Throwing.ino X
robotic arm course > 1_Servo_interface > 1b_Object_Throwing > 1b_Object_Throwing.ino >
  5    Author  : Muhammad Luqman
  6    Date    : 15-10-2020
  7    License : MIT
  8
  9   */
 10
 11
 12   #include <ESP32Servo.h>
 13   const int servoPin1 = 18;
 14   const int servoPin2 = 5;
 15   const int servoPin3 = 17;
 16   const int servoPin4 = 16;
 17   //ultrasonic sensor pins
 18   const int trigger = 13;
 19   const int echo = 15;
 20
 21   int motor,angle;
 22   long duration;
 23   int distance;
 24
 25   Servo servo1;
 26   Servo servo2;
 27   Servo servo3;
 28   Servo servo4;
 29   void setup() {
 30     Serial.begin(115200);
```

That is the main purpose, including the library. It is under the Amitay license. Wow. Read the angles and make the robot throw the object. This is an object of discord. So lame. Define the servo motors defined to new pens that are triggered an echo. We have worked with the ultrasonic sensor. These are the pens of the ultrasonic sensor. So much the duration and distances are also the variables for the ultrasonic sensor. What I'm trying to do is I will place a hand in front of the ultrasonic sensor and it will grab the object sort of. If I'm working and the robot comes to me, I place an object inside the clause. I say close the clause and throw the object. So the process of seeing the robot start working is the ultrasonic sensor, reducing the distance between the hand and ultrasonic sensor or placing an object in front of the ultrasonic like obstacle detection we did in mobile robotics.

```
int distance;

Servo servo1;
Servo servo2;
Servo servo3;
Servo servo4;
void setup() {
  Serial.begin(115200);
  pinMode(trigger, OUTPUT);
  pinMode(echo, INPUT);
  servo1.attach(servoPin1);
  servo2.attach(servoPin2);
  servo3.attach(servoPin3);
  servo4.attach(servoPin4);
  get_in_position();delay(3000);
}

void loop() {
  get_distance();
  if(distance<10){
    throw_object();
  }
}

void get_distance(){
```

So creating objects of the servo motors in the setup function, we begin to see little monitor defined the input mode and output of the pins of the ultrasonic sensor. Like we want to send the ultrasonic wave and then we receive it. So we have to define them in setup. What is any other function? Several motors are connected to the pins, the connection of the library, and the pins. Then we say get in position and delay for three seconds. What is this? It is a function called we do to make the robot take a specific position. And we say when the robot is in this position-specific position that is going to be represented in dysfunction, then rest for the three-second delay. Is that for that purpose? Let's first take a look at the function, get in position, get in position. It just makes the robot come to a certain position that I've made by hitting trial.

```
digitalWrite(trigger, HIGH);
delayMicroseconds(10);
digitalWrite(trigger, LOW);
duration = pulseIn(echo, HIGH);
distance= duration*0.034/2;
// Serial.print("Current Distance = ");
// delay(500);
// Serial.println(distance);
}
void get_in_position(){
    //get to holding position
    servo2.write(50);delay(500);
    servo3.write(50);delay(500);
    servo4.write(15);delay(500);
    servo1.write(0);delay(1000);
}

void throw_object(){
    //hold the object
    servo1.write(30);delay(1000);
    //move towards the bin
    servo2.write(150);delay(1000);
    servo3.write(0);delay(1000);
    servo4.write(60);delay(1000);
    //Drop the object
```

Fifty of the second motor rotating fifty of seven, three, fifteen or four and zero degree of sort of one and giving delay. So when one takes action they give a delay move and then it gives a delay, then move the last one, give a delay to make some sort of smoothness. But it was not I was not able to achieve smoothness with this delay. This way of giving delay was not suitable. We are looking to the advance and good version of this to give delays and make a smooth movement. So get in position is just giving angles to the motors and giving delay in load. The main thing that is happening, which is to obtain a distance and throw the object. What is intuition? We have to measure the distance to close the floor and start acting. So it is sort of if I am not giving anything to the robotic arm, don't keep moving on. If I give an object to the clause in between the clause, then take an action. OK, don't be like a mad thing or something like that. If I give an object and say the distance is less than ten or any condition less than ten centimeters, then start moving. OK, before that, don't move. That's the main thing that I want to achieve with this condition in the true object.

```
void get_in_position(){
  //get to holding position
  servo2.write(50);delay(500);
  servo3.write(50);delay(500);
  servo4.write(15);delay(500);
  servo1.write(0);delay(1000);
}

void throw_object(){
  //hold the object
  servo1.write(30);delay(1000);

  servo2.write(150);delay(1000);
  servo3.write(0);delay(1000);
  servo4.write(60);delay(1000);

  servo1.write(0);delay(3000);

  get_in_position();
}
```

What is happening, is almost the same, this same like getting in position because we are just giving angles with delays to make a robotic arm move because of how the robotic arm is moving, multiple joints are rotating. Currently, this is the basic chord. So a robot does not know anything about the location of its effect, which is an important thing. So let's take a look at it. It's called.

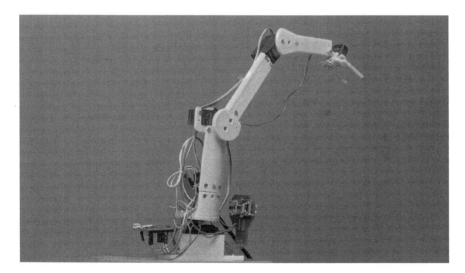

OPTIMIZE ROBOTS MOTION

Now, here, the problem is very serious, the robot is moving so fast, we have to slow it down somehow. Let's try how we are going to do that. Several motors and all of the motors are working on pulses or even we know what is probably from the 101 mobile robotics.

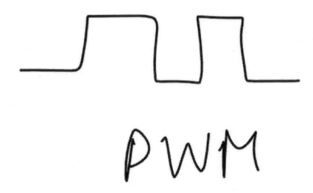

Now, B.W. signals are there are certain duty cycles. The periods and the frequency we are going to increase. The periods are duty cycle decrease to meet several motors a bit slower. And I think it is a difficult task. And currently, I think we have to make certain changes in the library to make it more slowly, or let's take a look at what I'm going to do. Now we are going to optimize our previous process of programming, a robotic arm. We are going to introduce smooth movement in our robotic arm and how we are going to do that. It's a quick look into it, and that is just introducing a for a loop. OK, simple for loop and how far loop can be so powerful. Let's take a look here. Allcott is similar to the previous cords, but we are going to just look into the loop and that is we have to loop it till the given angle.

```
robotic arm course > 2_Smoothing > 2a_Smooth_drive_Serial_Servo > C+ 2a_Smooth_drive_Serial_Servo.ino
23    Servo servo4;
24    void setup() {
25      Serial.begin(115200);
26      servo1.attach(servoPin1);
27      servo2.attach(servoPin2);
28      servo3.attach(servoPin3);
29      servo4.attach(servoPin4);
30
31    }
32
33    void loop() {
34      if (Serial.available() > 0) {
35        String first  = Serial.readStringUntil(',');
36        String second = Serial.readStringUntil('\0');
37
38        motor=first.toInt();
39        angle=second.toInt();
40        if (motor == 1){                    (const char [18])"Driving Servo 1 "
41          Serial.println("Driving Servo 1 ");
42          for (int pos = 0; pos <= angle; pos += 1)
43          {servo1.write(pos);delay(15);}}
44
45        if (motor == 2){ Serial.println("Driving Servo 2 "); for (int pos = 0; pos <= angle; pos += 1) {servo2.wri
46        if (motor == 3){ Serial.println("Driving Servo 3 "); for (int pos = 0; pos <= angle; pos += 1) {servo3.wri
```

OK, one, two, three, four, four degrees. So when we say one and then we count two before counting two, we have to give a delay in between. So it was like we give fifty degrees to a robot and the robot was moving so hot to 50 degrees. But now what we are doing is zero. One, two, three, four, five, six, seven. And then. It is now iteratively moving towards the exact angle that we are going to tell our robot, which is going to make smooth movements, increase the delay, more smooth movements. But there is a problem in this code that I want you to point out. What is the problem here? It will make the robot move smoothly, but you have to find out the problem. Let's take a look at the output of this code and understand.

TRANSFORMATION MATRICES

This portion is a mathematically, computationally expensive one, and theoretically, yes, as well, because we are going to understand some concepts of linear algebra as well, how we can explain our robotic arm in the words of linear algebra and maths. So starting with what is underactivated, I guess I have talked about earlier, our robot is three-degree freedom of robot. OK, three-D or F now you're robotic arm will be underactuated until unless it possesses six degrees of freedom because a robot can achieve a certain point with the limits of the length and joints of a robotic arm to a certain point in X, Y, Z. But we cannot achieve that point with all possible orientations in the 3D space. OK, that is why the robotic arm with less than three-six degrees of freedom is known as undereducated robotic arms. Then comes the point of Cartesian space. Cartesian space is just a name, a more mathematical name of X, Y, Z coordinates. These are Cardinia Cartesian coordinates, X, Y, Z, in which we represent the position of the robot in mobile robotics. We represent the position of the robot in this Cartesian space. Then comes the joint space will come to the joint space after we understand what kind of mics are OK, because it is a bit related to joint, obviously, but it would be easy to represent when we understand the forward of the concept transformation matrix. These mattresses are the most important and robotic arm. So what are those in transformation matrices? Let's say we have an axis here. I guess I can draw a tree there. Yes, this is let's make it a bit smaller. Yes. X-axis here, negative x-axis here, obviously Y-axis here and Z X is here. Now I see that I have another point which is here and then I have another point now. What is the point of the transformation matrix? This is the main one is known as the reference frame. OK, we have to explain all of the parts of the robot with the respect to a reference framework, which is at Origin mainly we call it the base frame and we use it to reference other frames. What is the position of frame number 10 concerning the base frame? So that is why we use the base frame to represent the position of other frames? This is the origin. What I mean by origin is the value of X is zero, the value of Y is zero, and the value that is zero. OK, that is known as the origin of simple maths. So if I want to find the location of this point, I have to draw a certain transform of that point from the origin. OK, I have to draw. What I'm saying is to find the location of this point in 3D space. I have to find a transform this green dotted line representing the next performing example to understand it better. So this is zero of all these three things. X I see, I see that movie we moved ten units, OK, ten units and in Z we moved seven units. And in X we don't have to move to get to the point E I'm calling it A. So what is the transformation matrix here? The values in the transformation matrix that are important to explain this concept are going to be enough for a cross for Matrix. That is the transformation matrix. And I would say there are two parts to the transformation matrix. The first one is currently having an identity matrix value you. Anything multiplied by this will be equal to that ten. OK, so that the thing that is multiplied OK portion, which is the translation part and we have an X, how much the difference between an origin. It is zero in a. Y-axis, it is 10 units, I'm obtaining these values and it is seven units. This is the transformation matrix going from which means if we want to go from origin to point eight to this point, following this line, what is the transformation we have to do in our to reach point eight? This transformation is the change we have to do to get to the point. So currently we have only the translation part here and the other part that is very essential, which is the orientation part.

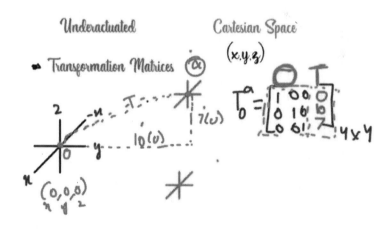

The rotational part is how much the point is rotated concerning the reference frame, obviously, but we are not going to be getting into the detail of the rotation part, OK, because we are not using it in this one-on-one. So for your just knowledge, the rotational part of the transformation matrix, this first blue box, contains all of the rotation exhortations via rotation, alongside axis rotation, the role picture of the point that we have to transform to get to the point. OK, but we are not dealing with that right now because iRobot isn't directly recreated. But still, we can rotate to three degrees. But again, we are not doing it in discourse. So we are going to stick with the translation origin. The point is we have this transformation. Now, if we want to go to point number B, which is this point and it has an axis around it, OK. So we say that this point here, having a distance from origin envie it is eight units and an X, OK, it is hard to represent a 3D concept in 2D, but let's assume this is a long X, OK, this is X and it is 17 X again, seven and X and inside it is the same as the origin. OK, this point is at the same location at this point, just translated in X and Y. What is going to be the transformation matrix from zero to be. It is going to be a game. We are not looking and looking at any rotation and we say that the orientation is the same as the origin. There is no rotation, just having some translations. OK, so the translation and X is seven units and it is eight, and in Z it is zero. There would be any Z translation I would have written hit. This is just to give you an example, how to write a transformation matrix and to further clarify the concept, why do we need it? So this is how we are going to write the transformation matrix. But what if we want to find a relation between this A and this B point? This line here represents a transformation that is unknown to us, that is unknown to us. But still, we can use this transformation desirability zero eight to find that relation, which is D, a, B, but how we are going to do that, this is going to be interesting. The formula for it is the E zero into the zero. B, the result is to be we don't have those things on the right equal sign. That is a zero. We have D zero eight but we do not have the zero. The thing that I want to just show you here, we can find the D?? by this formula, which is we have to have these two terms, same when multiplying and we can have this output. OK, if we have to thero here and we have to find the e0, we have to do an inversion of that matrix transformation matrix and that should follow the linear algebra conditions as. We can do that. But what is the point of all this? Why do we need it? So let's have a robotic example here.

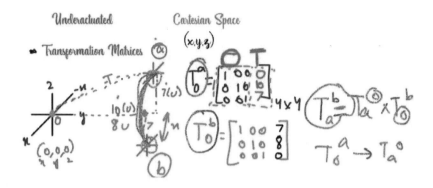

UNDERSTANDING THE APPLICATION OF TRANSFORMATION MATRICES

Let's say we have a robotic God. I'll try my best to draw the best God I can, but I think I've failed again. OK, we have another God. Here it is. Oh, I'm bad at trying things. And we have a camera here. This camera is looking at both of the cars and finding the distance of the cars. OK, it's sort of surveillance. So we know the transformation from God to the camera God Aleksic, which means the sea. And we know the transformation from this camera to the second car, which is DCB. OK, and with the help of a camera, let's assume we were able to find the position of our cars. OK, possession of the car with the help of just the camera images and we know the transforms as well. So what we are going to use the transform sword transform here is going to be used to find the position of the car number. Be concerning an as this transform from B is going to be found with the help of this multiplication that is DCB. And after having the results, what we are going to know, one God, the eCard is going to understand what is the current position of God? No, BSI cannot collide or I can somehow develop a swarm technology sort of that one robot knows about the second robot and they work in groups to perform a certain action. But that's all the next-level theory. But the thing is, you can find things concerning the origin of the base or the one thing that you have said for references and you can use it to do high-level tasks. Now it's time to get back to the point of robotic arms, right. We have a robotic arm here having multiple joints in it. I'll draw the joints with the black ink and we have multiple joints here in the robotic arm we have right now. I always mess up with the claw. The thing is, we want to find the end effective position in X, Y, Z. That is what we want. And we have a reference point here. With the help of transforms, we are going to do that and how we are going to first do that. We know with the help of this link that the transform from zero to one. This is one, this is two and this is three. We are going to save, you know, the transform from zero to one, from one to two, and two to three. We know this transforms. How much is the length and rotation of our actuators? These lengths are going to be the major thing that will tell us about the transform. And we want to calculate this magical relation from origin to the midpoint of our Glau and X, Y, Z with the help of transforms, we are going to do that. What is going to be the equation? D or three is going to be the zero one and two Done, two, and two. These two, three, that is going to result in two or three and people. This is known as forwarding kinematics. We were moving around this word forward kind of matics, especially kinematic. There are simple forward kinematics and inverse kinematics. The thing that forward kinematics tells us about is the relation of joint angles. With the help of joint angles, we find the Cartesian coordinates, OK, X, Y, Z. The next thing that is very important and robotic arms is the inverse kinematics, which tells us the opposite relation of our animatics retail Cartesian coordinates, and it tells us about the joints of our robot actuators angles. So why go forward? Kinematics is important. It is the first step to sort of do the thing that we did in the mobile robotics about localization, finding that y Cartesian space coordinates for a robot, and in the robotic arm, we perform forward kinematics to find out the X, Y, Z, Corton Cartesian coordinates. What I want here and what we will get is we will tell the robot what are the rotational angle theta one, two, two, and two to three. These three angles of this joint. I want to add to that three, the angles of these three joints as it is a trigger, or if this is the restaurant which is not considering the degrees of freedom and we will obtain it will tell us about the X, Y, Z of the end effector. Where is the end-effector? And you are building this intuition on how we can use the robotics forward kind of animatics to perform ACNC action. TNT is all about X, Y, Z, OK, and we can do that with favored candidate X of a robotic arm. And now we are going to implement the first one the of kind of medics forward kinematics then. Second, do you have contributive forward kinematics for a robot? And understand how we can use mathematical formulas to make a representation in Cartesian space. One interesting and important thing is it's not just this multiplication and we are not going to be doing this multiplication, because if we perform this whole multiplication of transforms, multiplying the multiplying, then what happens? We obtain a formula, a matrix that contains that thing that I told you earlier, a first-year rotation matrix and then a translation matrix, OK, in translation and rotation, both are both carry the cause and signs and lengths of that robot and a lot of trigonometric things. But what mattered to us is just the translation, remember? So it is also going to contain cause and signs and all three and even half single theories of trigonometry and a lot of stuff. But we will use those equations that we will drive with the help of libraries and implement them in our code. So then we will see as it should reach the point in the X, Y, Z. Is it reaching or not? We are going to test it and that end of that test, of course, will be ended. So talking just about the inverse kinematics in a very short period, we're not going to implement inverse kinematics, but let's talk about it in kinematics is the most essential thing of robotic arms because we just still go to this point and it sends the signal. It computes the signal. It computes the joint angles and sends that to the joints of the robot to move in such a way that the end effect to reach that point in forwarding kind of matics, we just tell the joints to rotate this much, this much, this much. And then the there will be at this point, forward kinematics is not that much use for that comparison to inverse kinematics in which we move the robot to the extend Vitan and it will automatically adjust the rotation of the motors and move to that point, which is more practical.

And Inveresk animatics is just not enough to make the robotic arm move perfectly. We have to plan the motion as well to move slowly, how to divide the steps, motion, planning algorithms. And that's why I'm not including that none or one. OK, it's now time to look into one representation of our robotic arm that is the d.H barometer and which we will use to give input to the library and that will produce the forward kind of magic solution for our robotic arm. Let's dive into the barometers.

INTRODUCTION WITH EXAMPLE

The representation, the now-retired on board representation of our robotic arm. This is a very common and initial stage that we do is to represent a robotic arm, its themes, its rotations, everything about physical, everything about robotic arm in a table that is disabled and with the help of people with using that table in libraries in Matlab to produce forward and inverse kinematics. OK, so this table is very important to understand. So let's start with just one example about that, a very simple one, which is this robotic arm. I know it does not seems like a robotic arm, but I want you to unlock the gates of creativity and imagination to understand it as we are going to say this thing, a robot. These are the actors and we are having, let's say, a top view, OK, to visualize things more and make things easy for each city in the U.S. And this is the first picture that this is the second and this is the third. The link between the second and third is a bit odd, but let's say let's go with it and solve it. So indeed, stable. The table is going to contain some headlines or some variables which will represent the robotic movement, its rotation. The first two things or the first two variables we are going to have are going to be Alpha and eight. OK, and finally, so we have three giants or keys, then we would have three entries in this table. Let's start with the first one, the first joint, its EXs or X-axis is represented here, this is the Z-axis before getting into details, Y-axis is not drawn because Y-axis is not used in these tables. It can be a floor. There are multiple floors of D triple representation. So for now there is no Y-axis X and Y and we are going to fill the table with the help of fixing Z-axis YSL, right. Sorry, X and Z for the second frame. X is here, Z is here, and for the third frame. Things are going to be different. I will not write it right now, so what are the values of Alpha? What is Alpha? Remember, these two things are dependent on ex. And said, OK, obviously, but more they are dependent on X, there are multiple explanations of the stable, but I will oversimplify things for you and make you understand more quickly regarding our problem. Our problem is not that complex to deal with all the properties of these tables. X-axis Elfa is the angle rotation around X-axis. So if it is X1, it is x2. Is there any rotation? How do we check it? We check with the respect of other X's like Zadik Scissored y-axis because if you did something around the Nexus that says it will be the same, I will be pointing in the same direction. So extraordinary. Next, do we have to relate both of these OKs in the next room? But for the first frame, what is important, there is a base frame that is on this frame, OK, that it can be below us as we are having a top view. So there is no difference in the first frame. And so in the zero frame by frame and the first frame. So we are going to say there is no rotation along X, there is no distance along the E x-axis. Along X-axis means there can be a translation between two successive x-axes. So in currently due to the base frame, there is no rotation and translation along X-axis in the second frame. What we are going to see, is there is any rotation in X1 and X2? Let's find out. With the help of other axes, both of the Z-axis, X1, and X2 are pointing upwards, which means X-axis is not rotated. If there would be a slight rotation, that axis of the Wozzeck two would not be pointing in the same direction as Alex Zone. So there is no rotation in X2 concerning X1.

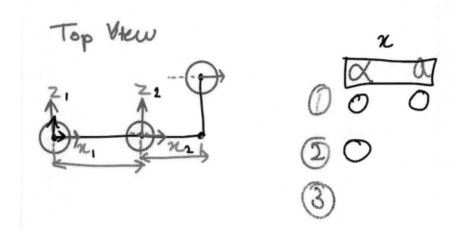

OK, is there a translation as X1 is a bit behind X2? So there is a translation and let's call that translation to be L1 and this is going to be a translation value of e a translation along the x-axis. OK, and everything is concerning the point here, the point at which the actuator is rotating. So this was zero-zero and that, you know, going to the next frame x3 is pointing in this direction and I am now going to draw something. And that is like this, this is Zugdidi, but this is not like this one. OK, it is hard for me to say that this is both the three and the two are not having the same direction because what I am trying to represent here is this is the same axis and it is not pointing upwards. It is going inside the Betacam for now. I have to draw the y-axis to represent it more accurately. If the y-axis was in this direction, if the y-axis was pointing in this direction for both of the previous axes, then the y-axis now is pointing upwards. Still, it's difficult. Y is pointing upwards and Z is pointing in the forward direction. OK, now from this point to this point, the points of now, the point of our frames, the middle point of A to where it is rotating these points on the x-axis. Let's take a look at both of the x-axis of these extra are pointing in the same direction. Find there is a translation in this Axis X1 an extra. Yes, there is. And we will call it to be x2 L2. Why I wrote to hit its 11-year-old to this is the translation along the x axis. Now the second thing is, is there any rotation along X-axis? If X two is here, X, Z two is pointing upwards in the next frame, Y is pointing upwards, heads are pointing upwards in the extreme three Y is pointing upwards, which means there is a rotation in that rotation is like this. If we have Z pointing upwards and X pointing like this, we rotated X in such a way that Z came to this point. So we have a rotation here and the rotation is not clockwise. Or clockwise, there are two options counterclockwise and anticlockwise, the rotation here at this point is clockwise. OK, all of our axes are rotating like this.

OK, all of the exits, the frames are rotating according to our actuator, which is pointing in the right direction, actuators are rotating on the Zadig in our representation. So this is the rotation that our motor is having on that specific point of entry at this point. And X-axis is rotated clockwise now, four. We like the angle to be negative and for the counterclockwise right angle to be positive, the value of alpha is going to be negative of 90. I know it is confusing, but it's completed. Now comes the major part. These were just two variables. There are other two variables as well. The Antigua and these two variables are mainly dependent on Z-axis, but we will be considered the X-axis as well as we did previously. And finally, what is D. D is counted along the Z-axis? OK, all of our X or frames are rotating along X-axis. X is also Residex. Z axes are pointing upwards. All of the links are rotating along with it. So there would be an angle in all of the frames. So to one t dart two and empty T for all of the frames D and technical part here in Zone and Z two, let's say for the Zone first Zone is compared with the base frame. Is there any translation in the Z Xs? No, it is not. The based frame is on the first frame so there is no translation in any X's and so we will write zero. But our concern is the Z-axis. Let's take a look at the second frame. Is there any translation in Z2 Axis compared to Zone, which means both of the frames are then translated to each other. A long Z 2x is. No, they are not. There are, they are translated along x2 x but not in Z Xs. So we will write zero here. Not looking at the third axis, is there any translation in the three axes as compared to the two. Yes, there is. And that translation is. This translation. Which I'm going to say three. This translation is a long Z Tiriac axis concerning this point of the two oh second frame. So I am going to write all three here, which concludes are deductible for this specific unknown shaped robot.

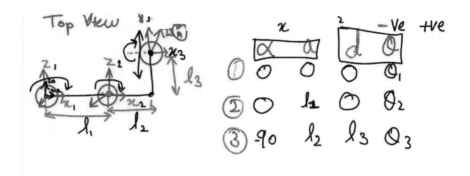

This is the way how we write this representation of a robot. And one interesting thing with this table, you can give to algorithms and it will calculate poverty and inverse kinematics for you. But this table should be correct.

DERIVING DH TABLE FOR OUR ROBOT

Coming to the Robot and CACO robot is a robot, this one which we are using and programming, we have designed it. So let's find a table for this robot. Right. There is a problem here in the drawing. Actuators are drawn from the two of you and there is a mixture of side views on top. So it will be a bit confusing, but I will try to solve it. OK, now the Xs on the upper Xs are y y-axis is pointing upwards on the upper actuators for the first picture to the basic to the desired dix's as upward as the base is rotating, this rotation is in this direction. And for these actually, the rotation is along this axis, which is coming out of the beach. So our Zedek says here is going to be in. OK, so we'll ride the tree here, their tree, and the one here, oh, what we have to do first compare the X-axis of consecutive frames, X1 and X2. Is there any translation along the x-axis of both of these frames? No, that is not an x-axis. That is translation. So we will write it to be zero. There is no translation along the x-axis. Is there any rotation along the X axis now? It's a rotation. So if you take a look, there is a rotation and obviously, Basslink is like this and the first link is like this. So obviously there is a rotation of this much, OK, just giving you an intuition. And that rotation is 90 degrees that were pointing upwards and now it is pointing out of the page. So there is a rotation of 90 degrees and mostly there is a rotation of 90 degrees. So it is 90. But what about the same? So the rotation from the base to the left one is in this direction. To me, it is counterclockwise. To you, it might seem to be clockwise. So that's why it is positive, 90 degrees coming to the next frame. Is there any rotation from this frame to this frame, second frame to the third frame, and there is no rotation along its axis of evil, right? Zero from this frame to this frame and effective frame to which a motor is connected that is connected. But we are not considering it to be a degree of freedom. It is just controlling the clock. So there is again, the frame seems y is pointing upward and X is here and that is pointing outwards. So there is no rotation along X-axis, so we will write zero E as the translation along X-axis. So from this point to x2 to the extreme is their translation. Yes, there is. And that translation is I will write it to be a two and one is this translation, the entry's this translation. So I will say a two is the translation along with x3 and then from X three to four, yes there is a translation and that is all three D now looking from frame number one to frame number two, I think things are here a bit messy, but we have to understand it. D There is a translation along. Zedek says that one X is and that is L1. Is there a translation of Z to access the three X? Is there a translation? No there is not butat pointing in the same direction and there is no translation from Z 2003, so there is no translation. Is there a translation from Z3 along with that three to Z four? No, there is no translation. Both are at the same points along the X-axis, so there is no translation in the Z-axis of the three coming to the rotation part. All have a rotation along that axis. So we will write to one to two and two-three. And this is our DH stable of Coccaro.

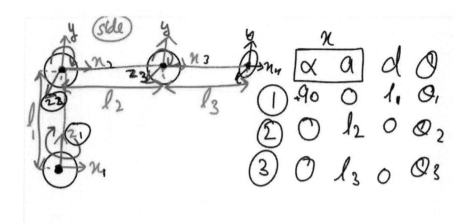

But this DHT representation is going to help us solve using libraries. We don't have to find the transforms and compute all of the multiplication in linear algebra to drive the equations. Libraries are going to do that for us, but you must understand how things work. You will not be able to get all of the knowledge of solving the DS stable. From these two examples, you have to look at complex storyboard systems for do you have sixty of you have to solve them.

1-DOF KINEMATIC ANALYSIS

Coming to the computationally expensive and hard part of this project, and that is kinematics, it is going to be the last, but it is very interesting and the learning curve is going to blow up. Simply theory was a lot. I know. Simple.

Cervelli attaching the suburban at this point we have to find only one suburban, and that is because we are going to use the first link, the base link that was vertical and that was just rotating on the A-Z axis is not going to be actuated, only distilling the second link is going to be actuated. So defining for several motor X and Y length of that link, twelve point five centimeters inside. We are defining the Siedel monitor and attaching the slope into the central object in the loop function. We are doing the same thing, obtaining an angle and giving the angle to the equations that we obtain from the library. This is the point where we are going to work a lot and on the output, I will show you how I obtain these angles. These angles are the main thing, right? Angle triangle, simple base hypotenuse, and perpendicular formula. Simple formulas are going to give us this equation, this X and Y equation. And you love how math is going to help us get this X and Y for a single link. OK, so then we will print and write the service and the service speed is at Max. Let's take a look. And its output. This is one deal. Everybody come, we are interested in finding X and Y by rotating this specific joint and it happens with the help of a triangle. The Seattle monitor says it should have twelve points five in X and zero in Y.

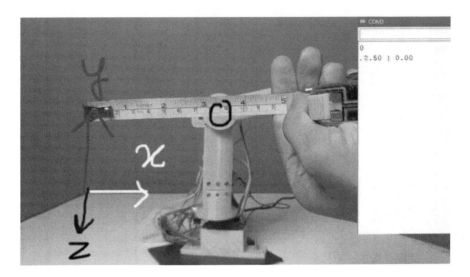

So you can see it is very close to twelve point five and X, but why is not zero? Because of the offset on the angle. OK, so let's give a 90-degree rotation. You can see and mathematically you can build the intuition that it should now make Y-axis as twelve points five and zero on X, but there is an offset that we should ignore for now to understand the concept. 160-degree rotation and it turns the eggs into negative eleven point seven five, so let's make it and we can see it is round about eleven points five, which is very accurate, but in the negative direction. So let's measure the Y-axis, which is produced to be four-point two, five, forward to seven. And if we measure it, we can see it is around about four point five.

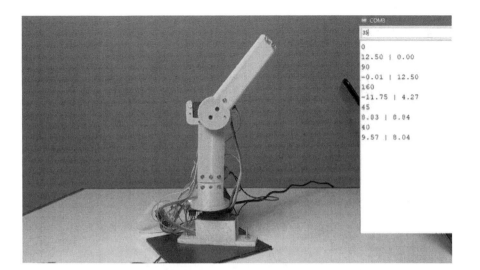

I think the values should be actual that by measuring hand there is some sort of very minuter at 35 degrees. It is ten points two for an X. Let's take a look at what we get on X. It is almost to be ten in X, so let's measure on the Y axis. What do we produce and what Arduino calculated values are are dissimilar or not. And you can see this one has a bit more error, sort of eight point five. So this is the output of what do you have, a robotic arm. And you can see the values are quite accurate. There is an offset that was producing some errors. What I think on whole results are accurate.

KINEMATIC SOLUTIONS THROUGH PYTHON LIBRARIES

Calculation of the forward kinematics equations and the way we are going to solve them, obtain them is a bit different from the basic workflow of the projects I have provided earlier because we are going to use Python on a cloud service of Google, that is Google CoLab. If you don't know about it, Google it. I will provide your notebook to you so you can make changes and develop solutions for your custom robots if you find this a little more black because I have applied the dark team as

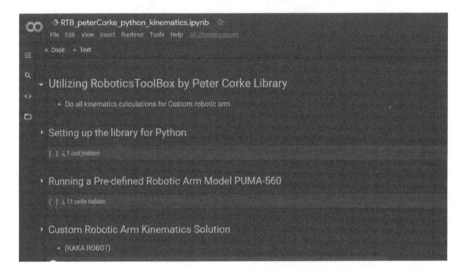

I like to work in teams, this file is going to contain different cells in which it will execute the python codes and obtain things from the servers. And a lot of things are going to be happening. But I have made everything very simple for you. So you just need to run the cells and you get the output. Isn't that good? OK, so the topic is utilizing Robotics Tool Box by Peter Clarke Library. This man, Peter Clarke, is awesome and he has made things a lot easier for us because if we get the kind of magic equations by just defining the parameters, it is awesome. Otherwise, we have to multiply different transforms and then a final expression and then solve a lot of things would be very hard for us in the form of 3D, three-dimensional computation. But petcock did a very good job and saluted this man. He made a library for Matlab as well as Python. But we are going to go with the Python library, OK, as Matlab requires a subscription and this is a free project, everything's utilized and it should be free. Right, except the hardware. OK, we are going to run this first cell, running it by pressing the button. It is going to download the library from the GitHub repository of Peter Clarke and then moving it into a certain folder and then installing the required things. But you just need to run this cell and it is going to do everything. Now, as we have installed it, libraries are all set, all dependencies are installed. We are going to work on this ORMA 560 as a robotic arm that is defined in almost all theoretical understanding books of robotic arms and sort of classic robotic arm. If we take a look here, BUMA 560 is this sort of robotic arm. You can see the structure. It is six degrees of freedom. The robotic arm on the robotic arm is to do it.

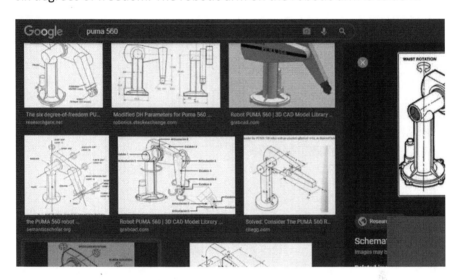

Remember the robot. But we'll use this robotic arm to understand the library, to build a basis because it is predefined, everything is predefined in the library about pumphouse. There are a lot of other predefined robotic arms, but sixty let's go with it. So we are going to import the library as RTV. If you don't know what is happening, we are using simple python syntax of importing the library and renaming it as AATB. So all of the functions of this robotics toolbox are available when we integrate the name RTV now the function is model and function. We are going to call the d.H barometers of Boomi sixty. They are already stored. So I'm going to run this cell and we are going to bring it to be 560 DS stable. The output is added stability dark alpha.

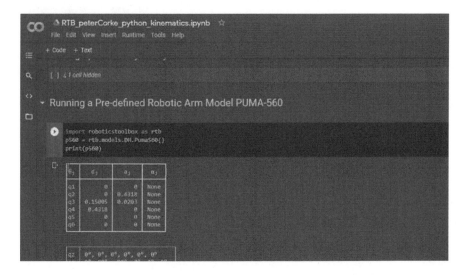

As you should remember, I told you in the one node explanation we have to define at the table before we proceed to kinematics things. So for PUMAR 560 things are defined here and library conditions are added robots as well. But the thing is, we are currently trying to understand how to forwork animatics can be obtained. We have the disease parameters. Let's write this function that is f fine, which is followed by kinematics running it.

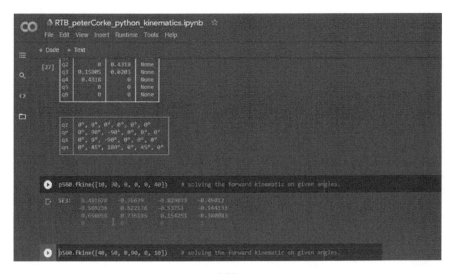

It produces a matrix that is not looking like a matrix, but it is a matrix and it is the transformation matrix. If you remember the red portions, the red-colored numbers are the rotational part of the matrix. The blue-colored numbers are a translation part of The Matrix. It is therefore gross for Matrix. It is a special occlude in space in 3D and it is a four-gross for Matrix. Now, what happened to be 560 was an object containing the [REMOVED] barometer. We use that as it was defined. V of the liability using that and called the function f Gingrich's calculative forward kinematics, we know that d.H barometer's said to calculate the forward kinematics, but what is the thing that we gave it and that was that were the angles in our case are the angles of the servo motors. Right? We get the angles. It produced the translation part. If we look at only the translation part, this is the value in X, this is the value envie and this is the value in Z, which means if we give five-sixty joint the servo motors, let's say if you have it, you give this angle to X actuators, your end-effector is going to be this X, Y and Z. OK, isn't that cool. It is calculating everything and telling us the answer is there are and there is going to be in the 3D space. This is so cool, by the way, if you don't found it now if we change the angles a little bit, what happens? The values changes. The rotation values are useful, but we are not utilizing them in this one or one project. So we are just looking at the translation part. We changed the values of the actuators and we obtain different results. We rotated the joints a little differently.

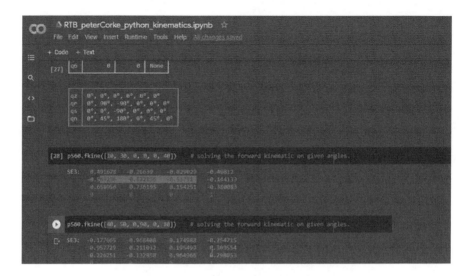

So I will be at a different point on set. Now, if you have more than 560 robotic arms and you have to code it, this is this process up to now is not going to help. You need certain equations that are going to be calculating the results. So you have to produce certain equations using this liability with the help of those equations that that those equations that this Efkan is using for the specified. Would you want those equations and you have to base them in your code. So your code, as I do know, ID code is going to tell you X, Y, Z when you give the angles automotives. Let's take a look at how we are going to do that. And that is going to be done with the symbolic library. Now, what is that as the symbol is a thing that is not going to change. It is not going to contain any value concerning programming. It is not going to change its value or it is not going to have any value. It is going to be just of just a symbol as we have equation X plus Y is equal to nine. Legacy to X is X and Y are symbols, X is equal to nine minus Y, this becomes an equation X and Y still symbols. There is no value for them. Let's take a look here. I have imported certain libraries obtained from the bitter cold notebooks that are very helpful. What I am going to do, again, is sort of importing the Pumar 560 model from the library. But this time I am going to say symbolism is equally true. This is not a thing that you should memorize. But just to give you an indication, symbolically, I have defined the angles of PI by two minutes by virtue. I obtained it, but by writing, just symbolic things are going to get symbolic.

OK, there are there is not going to be this type of solution with exact one floating. No, they are going to be huge equations that are not solved because they don't know about the value of the symbol like was like none. And now it is bye too. But this is not a very big difference. Right. Let's take a look at when the difference will become. So P 560 is going to give us exact values of transformation metrics because there is no simple and now we are going to create symbols. This line of code with the help of SIM, is this spatial Matlab but is going to create symbols. And with this ratio, we are going to create six symbols starting from zero. OK, but if I like you without any team, the cube will be printed if it is in the last line. So it is printed here.

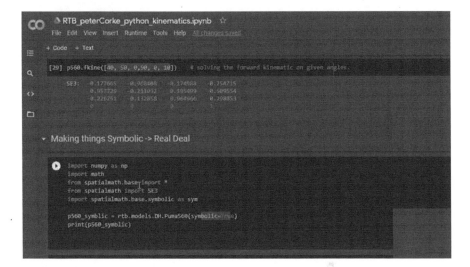

The SKU contains these six symbols. OK, this is important.

No running the next line that is going to calculate the forward kinematics based on those symbols previously. At this point, I like this place specifically. We were providing different angles for the Jones. Now we are providing symbols. So take a look at the output. It is huge output containing sine cause, angles, angles, and cost. And a lot of them are writing. A lot of them are blue. But The Matrix is so huge. Order is for growth. But still, there are a lot of equations with the sign cause and why it is like this. Because if I give the values of Q1, Q2, Q3 four to five, it is going to produce a result like this as we did earlier. But now I haven't provided the values of the angles six angles which are included in the computation of X, Y, Z of the end of the favored candidate X. That's why the gradient is so big that portions are traditionally part blue portions are retranslation. But the thing is, these are the equations that we wanted. But let's simplify them. I have ranked this cell that is going to simplify a little bit, solving raise them in good looking matrix form.

Now you can see they are good-looking, but still, the equations are numerous. This last column is containing the translation part. The first equation is of X. The second equation is so why the third equation is for Z in the 3D space for that. OK, let's extract the translation part and this is the translation part we are interested in PUMAR Now, if you had the tumor 560, you can write this in Arduino code and obtain X, Y, Z for the end affected.

You are just going to input the angles that we use to give to the several mortars and we are going to obtain the value of the X specified value.

This is like these values, we are going to obtain them. So that was the thing with Boomi. Five sixty. Let's now move towards the Kakeru abort. That is the custom robot and the library has no detailed knowledge of that robot. So we are first going to create the d.h barometer's creating the structure of the robot with the help of the stable regive. If you take a look here. Oh, this nineteen point one is the links. Lenthall number one link length then fifteen point six nine links to and Link Trailered. What is happening here? We are pasting r d e l find Teda. You can see here the explanation of D. That you have to first, provided the second thing is Alpha, then three, and then there are a lot of other things as well. But we are going to just stick with these four variables. Now, we Bastida did stable here and restored every single entry in lengua, including three just as variables. Then what we did, we said these are the three links with the respective rotation and its barometer's you can see concatenate them, make them a serial link, and save them as a Coccaro board. So at this point, the Coccaro board is actually if I run, it contains a complete description of this robot, OK, concerning its relation, concerning its length, length. And you can see robotics, toolbelt robot, D.H Better d.H Robot, which is this robot library. Understand, this is a robot with the help of the d.H barometer's, which currently we are not using symbols. Right. You have to remember this. We are just using exact values for the Lenglen and it is going to produce one simple transformation metrics that is not going to contain an equation. So what I'm going to do is run this cell. And this cell is producing results that I said gradational part and translation part, the input I gave is rotating the first motor, 60 degrees in the second zero degrees, the third 10 degrees.

Custom Robotic Arm Kinematics Solution

- (KAKA ROBOT)

```
[36]  ## creating Robotic arm through defining links and Serial Linkage
      Link_1=rtb.DHLink(19.1, math.pi/2, 0, 0)
      Link_2=rtb.DHLink(0,     0,    0, 15.69)
      Link_3=rtb.DHLink(0,     0,    0, 11.7)
      Kaka_robot= rtb.DHRobot([Link_1 ,Link_2,Link_3])
      Kaka_robot

      <roboticstoolbox.robot.DHRobot.DHRobot at 0x7fa41f289cc0>
```

```
T=Kaka_robot.fkine([60,0,10])
T
```

```
SE3:   0.799143  -0.518133  -0.304811   -5.50339
       0.255758  -0.185823   0.952411   -1.79011
```

And it produced that. You're a factor of the Coccaro. What is going to be of minus 5.5 and X minus one point seven nine envie and twelve point seven five seven three five in the Z-axis? And after we will be completing everything, extracting the equations from that, you can verify your answers with it. OK, now let's move to the part where we have to implement things, where we obtain equations so we can implement them in the Arduino code and we'll start creating let's start creating a Rikako robot with the help of symbols in which we give links as symbols. We don't give the values of the links. So we produced four symbols starting from one and save them in the capital. L named as a one or two and three. These are the links as symbols. Then we pasted the same DHT, but now we replace the values with symbols and L zero capital zero is L1. Then I'm going to name this robot Coccaro, but symbolic so you can differentiate. If you make changes, you can see the result now creating more symbols Q1, Q4, Q1, Q2 to Q3. OK, and these are the joint angles we are now going to give. Join Tango's named as Q1 and Links lenth named as well. They are going to be as symbols and they will be given to the system to solve our kinematics and we are now going to do that here. Let's see what happens again. We obtain a huge matrix blue translation Bartrop part rotation part. This is one of the best things that I can say Peter Clarke did because it was really hard to differentiate between translation and rotation in such a big matrix. Now, the thing is, Matrix is giving us the implementable equations, OK, that we can write in our code and we can get X, Y, Z when we provide the joint. Engle's OK, expensive than Vector Richton. Let's simplify it a bit more by just writing these three lines. In the third line, M is going to bring the Matrix M OK. And it has solved a lot by the way, not a little bit a lord. This is the total length of the Matrix and the previous matrix. You can see it was huge. Now this fourth column, this fourth column here is the translation part of the column right now, the translation part of the transform. Right. So we are now going to extract it. And you can see this translation part is what we are going to use and implement in our original board. If we compare it with the nonsymbolic thing, you can see the difference, the value, the values that are given, the results are produced, but they are not useful for the practical implementation. But when we get to a point where we want equations, we give things symbolically joined Engle's the Langlands and we produce equations. Then we again, I simplified them a lot. And these are the final equations that we are going to use in our code when we are going to implement it to be three degrees of freedom robotic arm, although I will be making things easy. So by dismantling the robotic arm, what degrees of freedom, two degrees of freedom, and then the three degrees of freedom. So you understand a little bit what is going on as we are not going into detail about how the kind of attacks are calculated by transformation, matrix, multiplication, and rotation things. But just an inside here, this minus six point one-two into the next one, minus seventeen, that's a hugely small number. So anything, let's say multiplied by zero. So we neglect these terms which are multiplied with so many small numbers, and then we write it with the remaining equation.

[Screenshot of a Colab notebook showing:]

```
M[:3,3] # extracting translation part

Matrix([
[-6.12323399573676e-17*L_2*sin(q1)*sin(q2) + 1.0*L_2*cos(q1)*cos(q2) + 1.0*L_3*cos(q1)*cos(q2 + q3)],
[ 1.0*L_2*sin(q1)*cos(q2) + 6.12323399573676e-17*L_2*sin(q2)*cos(q1) + 1.0*L_3*sin(q1)*cos(q2 + q3)],
[                                                    1.0*L_1 + 1.0*L_2*sin(q2) + 1.0*L_3*sin(q2 + q3)]])
```

OUR FINAL RESULTS TO IMPLEMENT IN CODE

- X = L_2cos(q1)cos(q2) + L_3cos(q1)cos(q2 + q3)
- Y = L_2sin(q1)cos(q2) + L_3sin(q1)cos(q2 + q3)
- Z = L_1 + L_2sin(q2) + L_3sin(q2 + q3)

Then you can see X is this, why is this? And that is this. We are going to write them in the original code and that is known as the implementation of our kind of matics. Let's take a look at what happens when we have one degree of freedom. What we calculate for our animatics, which will bring that factor to the ex-wife of space to this space, but the angle is going to be the main thing on which everything is dependent. Let's take a look.

IMPLEMENTING FORWARD KINEMATICS 2-DOF

The second chord is going to be interesting as we are going to introduce some more complex mathematical equations obtained from the forward kinematics result.

```
static const int servoPin1 = 17;
static const int servoPin2 = 16;
int servos_angle[2];
Servo servo1;
Servo servo2;
double x,y;
float l_1= 15.6; l_2=11.7;  in centimeters
void setup() {
    Serial.begin(115200);
    servo1.attach(servoPin1);
    servo2.attach(servoPin2);
}

void loop() {
    if (Serial.available() > 0) {
        String first = Serial.readStringUntil(',');
        String second = Serial.readStringUntil('\0');

        servos_angle[0]=first.toInt();
        servos_angle[1]=second.toInt();
        // input radians so converted degrees to radian first
        x=(l_1 * cos(servos_angle[0]/57.26) ) + (l_2 * (cos(servos_angle[0]/57.26 + servos_angle[1]/57.26 ) ));
        y=(l_1 * sin(servos_angle[0]/57.26) ) + (l_2 * (sin(servos_angle[0]/57.26 + servos_angle[1]/57.26 ) ));
```

OK, do servo motors or angles lens of the two lengths, I'm still the first. Basslink is stationary, OK, and attaching servo motors to the server up in the loop. We are waiting for the serial, but then when we get the serial input, we write the angles, the angles that we want the motors to date. We give them the angles to rotate and in return, we want what is the X and Y location of the end of activities, forward kinematics. And these equations obtain from the processing and programming and developing the help of libraries. We are going to obtain them and we have implemented them. One interesting thing that I did not discuss previously was this fifty-seven point two sixteen. This is convertor from degrees to radians. We give an angle in degrees, 90 degrees, 45 degrees, 30 degrees. We know we can visualize them easily, even I can. But the thing is, the functions cost function, sine function, and the trigonometric functions of Arduino Idy, get input in radians and process them. There is a reason, but I will not explain it all. You have to find it by yourself. But the thing is they require radion. The border thing here is happening. We are removing the robot at a slow speed. OK, it is not going to move relentlessly. The thing is this for looping thing with the delay and writing the angle iteratively has a problem. I think you might have found it by now. I've solved it. I will not solve it for you. OK, let's take a look at its output.

```
Co-ordinates calculated :   27.30 | 0.00
Co-ordinates calculated :   -0.03 | 27.30
Co-ordinates calculated :   6.01 | 22.95
Co-ordinates calculated :   27.30 | 0.23
Co-ordinates calculated :   27.30 | 0.00
Co-ordinates calculated :   7.83 | 11.66
```

Now we are going to have a duty of robotic arm, still, the first leg is not going to be actuated, but we are going to check the values of X and Y produced by the equations after giving the angles of the several mortars, which means we have a mortar and we obtained X and Y, but we want to check if they are accurate or not. So let's take a look. We give zero and it produced X and Y for X to be twenty-seven point three. And for the Y should be zero. There is an offset, as previously discussed. So it is twenty-seven point five, our physical results, and that is very close to the produced results from the equations. Now, let's give a rotation of 90 degrees on the first joint and you can see the X became the Y. What happens when we rotate along the Z-axis counterclockwise. So the left is going to be the same. Let's now give another rotation. So now let's give 50 to the first and sixty degrees to the second servo motor. And now let's measure first the Y value, which is twenty-two point nine five produced by the equations.

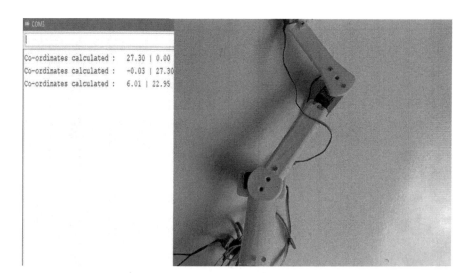

And we are going to cross-check with the physical results. You can see we obtain 22, which is very close to the actual results of the equations getting the values of the Y-axis and we obtain five point five, which has an error of very small value moving to the next rotation. I guess it is the second joint to be 113, the first to be ten degrees. So what is going to be the Y value and are measured by value is eleven point four or five and it is very close to the equation. Value the calculated value. The X value is seven points eighty-four equations and we obtain eight points one or two values. So our results are very accurate. Equations are working very fine. So the next step is three or four verticals.

IMPLEMENTING FORWARD KINEMATICS 3-DOF

Third, the gold of kinematics, the final part where we implement forward kinematics in our robotic arm, is going to be cool. It is under Amedee license. Nice. OK, getting the server library, attaching all of the pens involved in forwarding kinematics, obviously the FORTMAN is not involved. The last one is not involved, creating three objects, variable sorry, objects for the seven model, three lence of all of the links.

```
/*
 Date    : 14-10-2020
 License : MIT
*/

#include <ESP32Servo.h>
static const int servoPin1 = 5;
static const int servoPin2 = 17;
static const int servoPin3 = 16;

int theta_1,theta_2,theta_3;
Servo servo1;
Servo servo2;
Servo servo3;
double x,y,z;
float l_1= 19.1; l_2=15.69; l_3=11;7;  // in centimet
void setup() {

    Serial.begin(115200);
    servo1.attach(servoPin1);
    servo2.attach(servoPin2);
    servo3.attach(servoPin3);
}
```

And instead of being attached to several objects with the pins in the loop function with serial monitoring obtained angles for three servo motors, then we get converted from string to integer and then we conclude the forward kinematics put forward kinematics. We just need the integer value of the angles.

```
C 3_dof_kinematics.ino X
robotic arm course > 3_Kinematics > 3_dof_kinematics > C 3_dof_kinematics.ino > ۞ loop()
 32        servo2.attach(servoPin2);
 33        servo3.attach(servoPin3);
 34     }
 35
 36     void loop() {
 37        if (Serial.available() > 0) {
 38          String t_1 = Serial.readStringUntil(',');
 39          String t_2 = Serial.readStringUntil(',');
 40          String t_3 = Serial.readStringUntil('\0');
 41
 42          theta_1=t_1.toInt();
 43          theta_2=t_2.toInt();
 44          theta_3=t_3.toInt();
 45
 46          calculate_fk();
 47          print_XYZ();
 48          move_robot();
 49
 50        }
 51
 52     }
 53     void move_robot(){
 54        for(int pos=0;pos<=180;pos++){
 55          if(pos<=theta_1){servo1.write(pos);}
 56          if(pos<=theta_2){servo2.write(pos);}
```

It can be flawed, but we are dealing with integers because our library gets integers to calculate forward kinematics. Equations out here. Now this time we have a Z equation as well. OK, all of the three equations from the Forward Kinematics Matrix are implemented here. They seem to be a bit complex, but if you take a look at the fabric, animatics drive the equations from the library and these equations, they're the same. Implementation is a bit hard, which I have done for you. And now this seems good. They working. That's awesome. I've spent a lot of time on it to make them work. This fifty-seven point six, I am repeating it is to convert degrees to radians, OK, and then we calculate the forward kind of matics. Then we go to printing the X, Y, Z coordinate and then we move the robot and move the robot. We are going to again drive it slowly with the help of that idea for love with delays. There is a problem with it. I'm not solving it. OK, I bit of logic is involved here that I tried to run it OK continuously, but right only when the required angles are less than the amount that you are on and you can understand this condition easily and not a big deal. So I it is writing independently on all of the three objects of servo motor, the required several motors of a robotic arm. Let's take a look at its output, which is going to be more of measuring the things to get the X and Y, and Z accurately. How accurate equations are in producing results and how accurate and real-world our robot is moving. This is going to be interesting and I'm happy. For example, let's take a look. This is are going to be to you, everybody come, let's give a force rotation and start getting it. Here's the deal for you and we are going to do the major measurement. The first link is also actuated while meaning I made a mistake and place my finger on 25, although it was 27, nearly the Zedek says, which is important to us is at 20, which is very close.

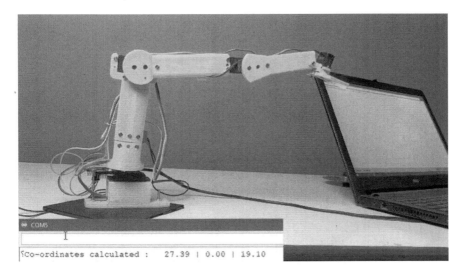

Now we are just going to measure the Z-axis after each rotation because we are only interested in that. This is the next state of our robot. Let me add the Z-axis and forty point file from equations and thirty-nine point five from real values to giving another rotation.

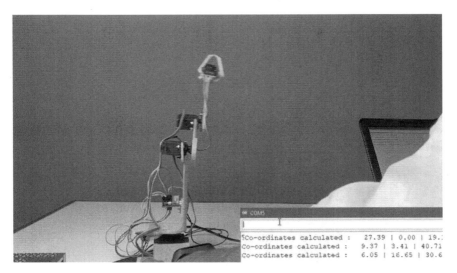

Here, the robotic arm is eight produced thirty point six two from the equations, and let's see what we got. It is 32, a bit blurry, but let's add thirty-one-point five. So iRobot Robot is producing quite accurate results and I'm very happy to look at these. Forward kinematics is solved for our robotic arm and it is working very fine.

ESP32 WIFI WEATHER STATION PROJECT WITH A NEXTION DISPLAY AND A BME280 SENSOR

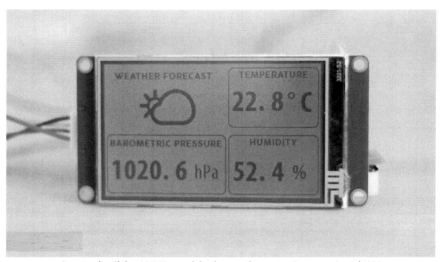

we are going to build a WiFi enabled weather station project! We are going to use the new, impressive ESP32 chip for the first time along with a Nextion display

we are going to make this. It is yet another weather station project I know, but this time we use the new ESP32 chip! We also use the new BME280 sensor which measures the temperature, the humidity, and the barometric pressure. When we power up the project, it connects to the WiFi network, and it is going to retrieve the weather forecast for my location from the open weather map website. Then it will display the forecast on this 3.2" Nextion Touch Display along with the readings from the sensor! The readings are updated every two seconds and the weather forecast every hour! As you can see, in this project we use the latest technologies available to a maker today! If you are a DIY veteran, you can build this project in five minutes. If you are a beginner, you have to watch a couple of videos before attempting this project. You can watch those videos by clicking on the cards that will appear during the video. Let's start! In order to build this project we need the following

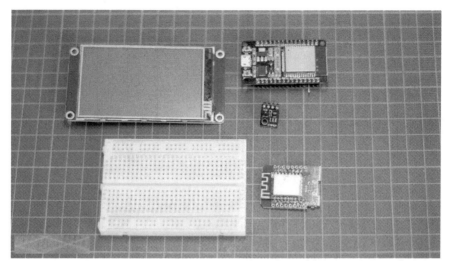

parts: • An ESP32 board • A BME280 I2C sensor • A 3.2" Nextion display • Some wires The cost of the project is around 30$. You can find links to the all the parts I use in the description of the video below. Instead of the ESP32, we could use the cheaper ESP8266 chip, but I decided to use the ESP32 to gain some experience with it and see what works and what not. This is the first project I ever build with the new ESP32 chip.

If you are not familiar with it, the ESP32 chip is the successor of the popular ESP8266 chip we have used many times in the past.

SPECS/BOARD	ESP32	ESP8266	ARDUINO UNO
Number of Cores	2	1	1
Architecture	32 Bit	32 Bit	8 Bit
CPU Frequency	160 MHz	80 MHz	16 MHz
WiFi	YES	YES	NO
BLUETOOTH	YES	NO	NO
RAM	512 KB	160 KB	2 KB
FLASH	16 MB	16 MB	32 KB
GPIO PINS	36	17	14
Busses	SPI, I2C, UART, I2S, CAN	SPI, I2C, UART, I2S	SPI, I2C, UART
ADC Pins	18	1	6
DAC Pins	2	0	0

The ESP32 is a beast! It offers two 32 processing cores which operate at 160MHz, a massive amount of memory, WiFi, Bluetooth and many other features with a cost of around 7$! Amazing stuff! It will help understand why this chip will change the way we make things forever!

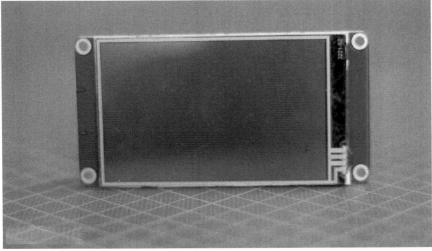

Also, this is the first project I build with a Nextion touch display. The Nextion displays are new kind of displays.

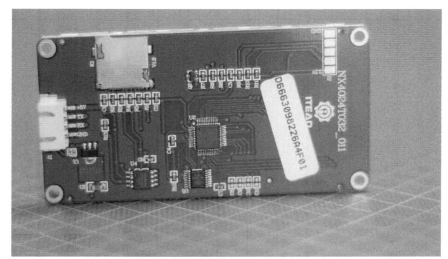

They have their own ARM processor at the back which is responsible for driving the display and creating the graphical user interface. So, we can use them with any microcontroller and achieve spectacular results. I have prepared a detailed review of this Nextion display which explains in depth how they work, how to use them and their drawbacks.

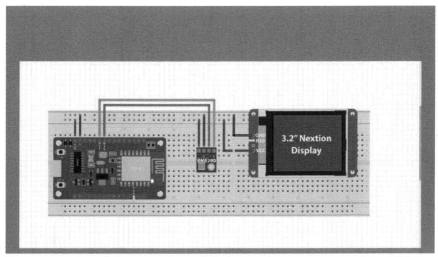

The connection of the parts is straightforward as you can see from this schematic diagram. You can find a link to the schematic diagram in the description of the video below. Since the BME280 sensor uses the I2C interface, we only need to connect two wires to communicate with ESP32.

I have attached the sensor to Pins 26 and 27. In theory, every digital pin of the ESP32 board can be used with I2C peripherals. In practice though, I found out that some pins did not work because they are reserved for other uses. Pins 26 and 27 function great! To send data to the display, we only need to connect one wire to the TX0 pin of the ESP32. I had to bend the pin like this to connect the female wire of the display since the ESP32 board is too big for this breadboard. After connecting the parts, we have to load the code to the ESP32, and we have to load the GUI to the Nextion display.

If you have trouble uploading the program to the ESP32 board, hold down the BOOT button after pressing the upload button on the Arduino IDE.

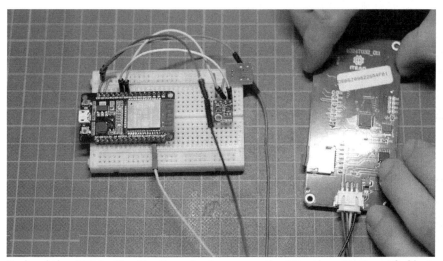

To load the GUI to the Nextion display, copy the Weather Station. tft file I am going to share with you to an empty SD card. Put the SD card into the SD card slot at the back of the display.

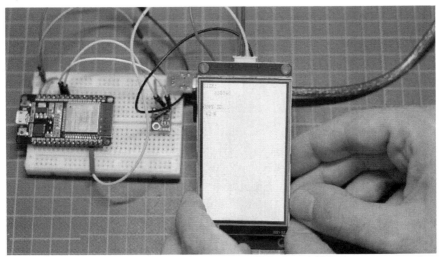

Then power up the display, and the GUI will be loaded. Then remove the SD card and connect the power again. After successfully loading the code the project will connect to the WiFi network, it will get the weather forecast from the openweathermap.org website, and it will display the readings from the sensor. Let's now see the software side of the project.

To parse the weather data, we need the excellent Arduino JSON library. We also need a library for the sensor. You can find links to all the libraries in the description of the video below. Let's see the code now. At first, we have to set the SSID and the password of our WiFi network. Next, we have to enter the free APIKEY from operweathermap.org website. To create your own API key, you have to sign up on the website.

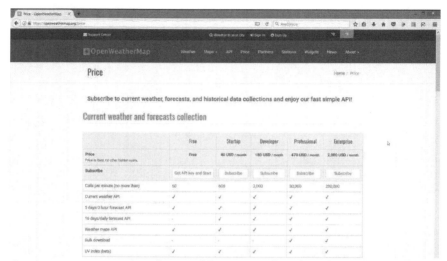

Getting current weather data and forecast is free, but the website offers more options if you are willing to pay some money. Next, we have to find the id of our location. Find your location and copy the ID which can be found in the URL of your location. Then enter your city's id in the CityID variable. Also, enter the altitude of your town in this variable. This value is needed for accurate barometric pressure readings from the sensor. Now we are ready to move on. At first, we initialize the sensor, and we connect to the WiFi Network. Then we request weather data from the server. We get a reply with the weather data in JSON format. Before sending the data to the JSON library, I manually delete some characters that were causing me problems.

```
145
146 result.replace('[', ' ');
147 result.replace(']', ' ');
148
149 char jsonArray [result.length()+1];
150 result.toCharArray(jsonArray,sizeof(jsonArray));
151 jsonArray[result.length() + 1] = '\0';
152
153 StaticJsonBuffer<1024> json_buf;
154 JsonObject &root = json_buf.parseObject(jsonArray);
155 if (!root.success())
156 {
157   Serial.println("parseObject() failed");
158 }
159
160 String location = root["city"]["name"];
161 String temperature = root["list"]["main"]["temp"];
162 String weather = root["list"]["weather"]["main"];
163 String description = root["list"]["weather"]["description"];
164 String idString = root["list"]["weather"]["id"];
165 String timeS = root["list"]["dt_txt"];
166
167 weatherID = idString.toInt();
```

Then the JSON library takes over, and we can easily save the data that we need in variables. After we have kept the data in variables, all we have to do, is to display them on the screen and wait an hour before requesting new data from the server. The only information I present is the weather forecast, but you can display more information if you wish. It all here saved in variables. Then we read the temperature, the humidity and the barometric pressure from the sensor and we send the data to the Nextion display.

```
43 }
44
45 void loop() {
46
47   delay(2000);
48
49   if(iterations == 1800)//We check for updated weather forecast once every hour
50   {
51     getWeatherData();
52     printWeatherIcon(weatherID);
53     iterations = 0;
54   }
55
56   getTemperature();
57   sendTemperatureToNextion();
58
59   getHumidity();
60   sendHumidityToNextion();
61
62   getPressure();
63   sendPressureToNextion();
64
65   iterations++;
```

To update the display, we simply send some commands to the serial port. If you get this compilation error while compiling, you have to add this -

fno-threadsafe-statics at the platform.txt file which is located here: ...
Press save, and then the project will compile fine. The software for the
ESP32 is not mature, yet so some things do not work at once yet.

The Nextion GUI consists of a background, some textboxes and a picture
that changes depending on the weather forecast. Please watch Nextion
display tutorial for more information.

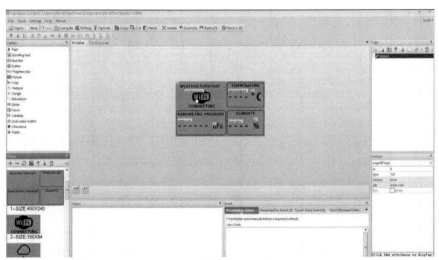

You can quickly design your own GUI if you wish and display more things
on it. As always you can find the code of the project in a link in the
description of the video. As you can see, an experienced maker today can
build exciting projects in just a few hours with a few lines of code and

only three parts! A project like this would have been impossible to make even two years ago! Of course, this is just the beginning of the project.

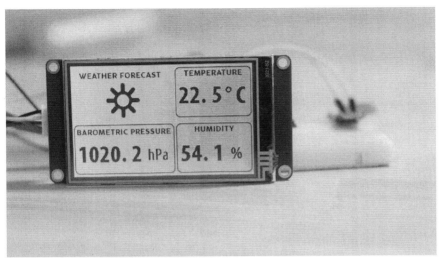

I would like to add many features to it, like graphs, touch functionality that is now missing, maybe a bigger display and of course a beautiful looking 3D printed enclosure. I will also design a better looking GUI and icons. I have some very fresh ideas to implement! I would love to hear your opinion about today's project.

THE END

Made in the USA
Columbia, SC
01 May 2025